Charles W Hemenway

Memoirs of my Day in and out of Mormondom

Charles W Hemenway

Memoirs of my Day in and out of Mormondom

ISBN/EAN: 9783743334410

Manufactured in Europe, USA, Canada, Australia, Japa

Cover: Foto ©ninafisch / pixelio.de

Manufactured and distributed by brebook publishing software (www.brebook.com)

Charles W Hemenway

Memoirs of my Day in and out of Mormondom

MEMOIRS OF MY DAY

In and Out of Mormondom.

BY

Charles W. Hemenway,

A JOURNALIST.

WRITTEN IN PRISON

While the Author was undergoing sentence for alleged libel.

SALT LAKE CITY, UTAH,
FEBRUARY, 1887.

TO

HIS WELL-BELOVED AND EVER AMIABLE WIFE,

IRETA,

THIS VENTURE OF HIS PEN IS

AFFECTIONATELY INSCRIBED AS A SLIGHT TOKEN

OF HIS GRATITUDE FOR HER COMFORTING KINDNESS, AND

IN COMMEMORATION OF

HER PERFECT FIDELITY AND HAPPY COURAGE

IN THE HOUR OF CRUEL TRIAL,

AS EVER, BY

THE AUTHOR.

PREFATORY.

It was not my intention to write a complete autobiography; neither was it my purpose to compose a learned or profound work when I undertook the task of writing this small volume. I have written merely to while away the dreary hours of confinement, and not with the idea of furnishing any very startling narrative from a life which has not yet numbered its twenty-seventh year. Incidentally I have recorded some passing recollections as they came to my mind, without any effort at embellishment. During the past two or more years prior to my incarceration, I edited a Mormon paper in Ogden, Utah, and in that capacity became somewhat familiar with the character and peculiar institutions of the Mormon people. My residence among them is adverted to merely as an incident in my experience, and not with any design to influence the solution of the Mormon question.

CHARLES W. HEMENWAY.

OGDEN, 1887.

CONTENTS.

CHAPTER I.
Birth and Parents.—An Overgrown and Awkward Boy.—As Book-keeper and Student.—Branching out in Poetry.—"Lourne and Lucadie."—Leaving Home.   Page 1

CHAPTER II.
Beginning a Pilgrimage.—A Veiled Female.—The Story of her Ruin.—At New York City.—Disregarding Formalities of Etiquette.—Among Jeweled Dames.—At Washington.—Congressmen not Demi-Gods.   9

CHAPTER III.
Short of Funds.—A Voyage to Rio de Janeiro, Brazil.—Homesickness.—A hasty Return.—Changed by Experience.—Penniless and Friendless in the Streets of New Orleans.   18

CHAPTER IV.
Not every Man that cares to practice his own Philosophy.—Adventures in New Orleans.   25

CHAPTER V.
Struggling with Fortune.—A lucky Sale of Manuscript.—Trusting to the Promptings of an inner Monitor.   32

CHAPTER VI.
Where Gen. Jackson whipped the British.—Col. Varres.—Again at Sea.—Conjugal Infidelity and Murder.   38

CHAPTER VII.
Forebodings.—Shipwrecked.—Coffined among Shells and Sharks.   45

CHAPTER VIII.
Adrift in Open Boats.—Dashed upon the Sand.—Through Mexico.—Señor Luna's Family.   53

CONTENTS.

CHAPTER IX.
To Guaymas.—In a Pest-house.—Saved by Sisters of Charity.—To San Francisco and Australia.—A Horrible Scene. 60

CHAPTER X.
Back to the Pacific Coast.—In Southern Arizona and New Mexico.—To the Sandwich Islands as a Secret Agent.—Eccentric Colonel Norris. 68

CHAPTER XI.
In Honolulu.—The Kanakas.—Ah Fong, a Chinese Millionaire, and his unfortunate Daughter. 75

CHAPTER XII.
Kauai.—Kapaa.—Colonel R. Z. Spaulding.—The Condition of Laborers in Hawaii. 81

CHAPTER XIII.
As a Spy.—A Christmas Celebration.—As Government Inspector of Roads.—Native Habits and Costumes. 88

CHAPTER XIV.
Before Hon. Rollin M. Daggett.—Editor of the *Advertiser*.—His Excellency Walter Murray Gibson, a Remarkable Genius. 94

CHAPTER XV.
Exceptional Opportunities.—Iolani Palace.—His Majesty King Kalakaua and Queen Kapiolani.—Punchbowl.—Laie, the Mormon Plantation. 101

CHAPTER XVI.
Coronation of King Kalakaua.—Among would-be Revolutionists.—Speech-making for his Life.—A Suicide. 109

CHAPTER XVII.
Maui and Hawaii.—Claus Spreckels and Spreckelsville.—Haleakala.—Kilauea.—The Legend of the Beautiful Hawaiian Princess. 116

CHAPTER XVIII.

Back again to Native Land.—Editor of the Salem, Oregon, *Talk*.—A Rustic journey to Baker City.—In Boise City, Idaho. 127

CHAPTER XIX.

In Utah at Last.—Payson a Place of Destiny.—In Love.—The Result. 134

CHAPTER XX.

Prove City.—Installed in the *Enquirer* Office.—Editor of the Ogden *Daily Herald*.—Married.—To Ireta. 142

CHAPTER XXI.

Some Account of Miss Ireta Dixon and her Family.—Utah Girls make Good Wives. 149

CHAPTER XXII.

A Sketch of the Libel Suits.—In Jail.—"Good Bye." 155

CHAPTER XXIII.

About the Mormons.—The Wonderful Religion of the Latter-day Saints. 169

CHAPTER XXIV.

Plural Marriage.—Miscellaneous.—Scenery.—Railroads.—Mining Resources 176

CHAPTER XXV.

The Mormon Problem.—Utah Courts.—Open Venire.—The Crusade. 184

CHAPTER XXVI.

Three Souls with but a single Thought; *Three* Hearts that beat as one. 192

CHAPTER XXVII.

A Symposium of Personalities.—Conclusion.—Au Revoir. 201

APPENDIX A. - - - 245
APPENDIX B. - - - 257

MEMOIRS OF MY DAY

In and Out of Mormondom.

CHAPTER I.

Birth and Parents.—An Overgrown and Awkward Boy.—As Book-keeper and Student.—Branching out in Poetry.—"Lourne and Lucadie."—Leaving Home.

AN old family Bible, stained with age and usage, contains the first record of the fact that Charles W. Hemenway was born in Makee township, Allamakee County, State of Iowa, on the 22d day of March, 1860. His parents were both born in the State of New York and they first settled in Iowa when that commonwealth was a Territory, inhabited chiefly by wild Indians. When the object of our sketch first saw the light his father was a farmer in good circumstances. He was then a strong, tall, vigorous man, with sandy or red beard and light brown hair which is now white as driven snow, for he is seventy-four years of age. He was never married but once, and the wife of his youthful choice still lives. This venerable man and his aged consort have passed a happy and prolonged existence together. They have had only two children. The first was a daughter, named Mary, born in 1840, and the second was, of course, Charles W. Hemenway. The daughter died in 1866, when the son was but six years old, and he has but a very vague recollection of his only sister. Some seven years before she died she was married to one Augustus K. Pratt, who turned out to be a very indifferent husband. When she died she left three children—two daughters and a son near six years of age. The daughters soon died; the son, Clinton Pratt, lived to reach manhood when he, too, died, leaving no family.

If the reader will go back to Waukon, a considerable village in northeastern Iowa, where Mr. and Mrs. Charles Hemenway, Senior, have spent most of their lives, he will find that their reputation for truth, industry, personal honor and rectitude is in every respect above reproach. The senior Hemenway's word is and always has been as good as his bond. He and his wife have been Methodists for many years, and they are devout and sincere in their religious belief, too. As parents they were kind and indulgent to a fault. Their son and only surviving child, Charles W., was reared with every possible tenderness. At an early age they placed him at school, and afforded him every educational advantage within their reach. They even sacrificed their own comfort frequently for his benefit and advantage.

In politics the elder Hemenway has long been a staunch republican, but he never aspired to office, and was altogether a modest, retired, sober, earnest man who avoided notoriety and detested display, and loved and practised virtue, honesty and simplicity. Even the breath of suspicion never approached his name. His wife was of a very similar nature—a true and devoted wife and mother, although for many years she was an invalid. To these kind and indulgent irreproachable parents Charles W. Hemenway owes whatever he may possess of manhood, courage and integrity. To him those parents are dearer than words can express.

In early youth the son was an overgrown, awkward boy. At the age of sixteen he was nearly six feet tall, and that is his height to-day. At the age of seventeen he had a mustache almost as long and heavy as that which he now wears, and his mind was quite as precocious as his body. At the age of eighteen he had completed his education at school, and during his eighteenth year he entered the employ of Hon. Willard C. Earle, the proprietor of a mammoth general merchandise establishment, and in less than three months became chief book-keeper and cashier. This position he held, to the entire satisfaction of Mr. Earle, until August, 1879. Prior to and during this time he accumulated a large library of standard works, which he read with care, often working all day at the desk and then sitting up until two or three o'clock in the morning with some noted author's work before him.

Until young Hemenway was nineteen years of age he never once attended any party or sociable to stay more than fifteen minutes. He cared little for the society of young people of his age and up to that time he had never played a game of cards, drank a drop of spirituous liquor as a beverage or visited the interior of a saloon. As a boy he was sent to Sunday School at the Methodist church, but as a young man he rarely attended divine service at all. People generally called him eccentric and dubbed him the "old man" because he took but little stock in the sports of boys, cared nothing for flirtation with the girls and courted the good opinion and society of his seniors and betters, besides applying himself to study and business incessantly.

Early in 1879, young Hemenway, then nineteen years of age, published a collection of his juvenile poems and lampoons, in book form under the title of "Lourne and Lucadie." This crude little volume contained several severe satires upon local preachers, deacons and politicians. It caused a wonderful degree of local excitement and discussion, and the young author woke up one morning and found himself not a little famous. About one half of the residents of his native village were soon about ready to throttle the other half, all because of his little book. Among others, the juvenile satirist had attacked the follies and foibles of Congressman Updegraff and Major D. W. Reed, both republican politicians of a petty kind, and as a consequence the republican paper of the village, and ultimately the republican press of the whole State, made war upon the young author, while the democratic papers generally and warmly defended him. From that time Hemenway has been a democrat. While this newspaper controversy was progressing, the little volume of poems sold like hot cakes and to his great surprise the author had his first edition speedily exhausted and his pockets replenished with cash.

In some instances he was assailed with the most atrocious libels and the Waukon *Standard,* a local republican paper, was so much irritated that it kept up its fusillade of abuse for four weeks, finally publishing a collection of its choicest smut-productions in pamphlet form with penny-a-liner comic wood cuts. This only advertised "Lourne and Lucadie" more than ever, and a new edition was demanded. While the newspapers were engaged in this discussion of the young man's book he was menaced with all sorts of threats from a horse-whipping to lynching, and his friends jealously protected him from the least harm. At the end of four or five weeks when the excitement had somewhat subsided he, for the first time, came to his own defense and published an article some seven columns long in the Waukon *Democrat* which won him a complete victory, and silenced his local enemies so effectively that they have remained silent ever since.

In those early years, Hemenway entertained a fabulous ambition. He cherished an all-absorbing desire to be an immortal of some sort, and his ideas of greatness were gathered from the characters and acts of all the chief heroes of history. Plutarch's "Lives," Rollin's "Ancient History," Guizot's "Napoleon and his Marshals," and Gibbon's "Decline and Fall of the Roman Empire," were his especial delight. But he devoured everything in the shape of literature that came in his way, only rejecting most works of fiction but including poetry, of course. The works of Goethe and Schiller, the great German authors, were also read with zest; the perusal of Carlisle's "French Revolution" marked an epoch in his intellectual life; the Bible, the Koran, Darwin's "Origin of the Species," "The Descent of Man," by the same author, and Tom Paine's and Voltaire's works were alternately read and studied.

Sometime in the year 1877, young Hemenway had reached the conclusion that he never could attain the height of his vaulting and of course chimerical ambition unless he could travel extensively among men in all parts of the world and observe for himself all that existed, as far as might be expedient or possible. Quietly and secretly he formed a determination to leave home and parents, and start out on a pilgrimage alone through the world, to fit himself for the sphere which he longed to occupy in life, by gathering the wisdom of experience and personal observation. To the end that he might undertake such a journey every subsequent act of his life, for a time, was made subservient. In order to raise sufficient money to start out with, the publication of the book "Lourne and Lucadie" was designed; and, as we have seen, it was a famous financial success. Indeed that little venture supplied him with all the cash he needed to launch himself out into the world. And soon after he had completed his nineteenth year he made the final preparations to travel abroad. Yet it was not until some time in August, 1879, that he finally resigned his position with Hon. W. C. Earle, bid adieu to his beloved and venerable parents and a host of kind friends who had accorded him extravagant homage, and then departed from the scenes of his boyhood, to try his fortunes among strangers, in a world full of hardships and pitfalls for the inexperienced traveler.

CHAPTER II.

Beginning a Pilgrimage.—A Veiled Female.—The Story of her Ruin.—At New York City.—Disregarding Formalities of Etiquette.—Among Jeweled Dames.—At Washington.—Congressmen not Demi-Gods.

> Ye gods who guard my Star of Fate!
>   Try me in storm and fire;
> And if I cannot live elate
> And win the nobler grand estate,
>   Let me in youth expire!

THUS runs a portion of a poetic prayer which emanated from the soul and was formulated by the pen of young Hemenway, long before he could have had any practical idea of the burdens, cares and grievous vicissitudes which even the noblest career of ambition must lead through, ere the world will concede the laurels of lasting and refulgent glory as an individual possession. And again, upon departing from the home of his childhood, when beginning a pilgrimage which was to consume over half a dozen years and end none could say how, the same sentiment—tinged with a romantic enthusiasm, and the love of adventure—made his pulse beat quicker and his hope soar into the realms of dreamland. At his native town of Waukon, he took the train alone one chilly afternoon and the next morning he was in Chicago; the following day he reached Detroit where the whole train was run upon a ferry boat and transferred over on to Canadian soil. While waiting at a station but a short distance from Detroit, an elderly gentleman, richly dressed, who had in his custody a young lady whose hands were securely tied, boarded the train. The couple took a seat directly in front of Hemenway. The young lady was dressed with great care and wore the most costly apparel. At first her face was closely veiled and altogether an air of mystery seemed to hover around her. After riding some distance she begged her male companion to remove the veil and untie her hands which was accordingly done. Presently she turned her face around. Never before or since have we seen such a wonderful countenance. Traces of great beauty were discernable in every lineament; a ghastly palor gave the face an unearthly appearance; her brow was high and broad; her eyebrows dark and arched; her eyelashes long and glossy; her eyes large, black and glowing with a wild and weird pathos which told only too plainly of a mind deranged and a heart broken. The passengers all stared at the unfortunate creature in blank astonishment. Hemenway gazed at her forlorn face a moment and when he turned away large tears were standing in his eyes—so easily and deeply was his heart moved to pity and to sympathize with the misery of even a stranger. He was also curious to learn the history of the ill-fated lady. When the train reached Niagara Falls an old woman boarded the train, and, quaking with emotion, came forward and embraced the unfortunate as her "dear daughter;" but that daughter stared in wonder and could not recognize her own mother. It was an affecting scene, and it made a deep impression upon the heart of the young pilgrim. We ascertained from the gentleman in charge of the wrecked young lady the story of her ruin. She was the youngest child of a wealthy retired merchant of Rochester, New York. She had been reared tenderly and educated carefully. Every care had been taken to protect her from the rude blasts incident to ordinary life; and, like a tender plant, she grew up among friends, nursed in the lap of luxury and devoutly beloved by all who knew her. But in an evil hour a despoiler came in the shape of a young Congregational minister, who represented himself as the heir of a vast fortune. He wore a fair exterior; his tongue was apt in prayer and sermonizing, and his appearance was pleasing and prepossessing. In due time he won the merchant's daughter and got into his hands her goodly dowry. Then he took her to Canada and after a few months' succeeded in breaking her heart by cruel treatment and debauchery, and eventually, to cap the climax of his villainy, after her fortune was trifled away, he deserted her in want and wretchedness and left for parts unknown. This was more than the young wife's mind could bear and her reason was hopelessly dethroned in an hour. Oh, God! how many thousands of such or similar cases are recorded throughout the Christian world each year? Why, oh why! are men so base and depraved permitted to live after they have worse than murdered those who loved them best and trusted them most?

Eventually Hemenway reached the great city of New York and he immediately became engaged in observing the sights, which all had the freshness of novelty to his eyes. To him the great metropolis was only a gigantic stage upon which the extended drama of life was being enacted perpetually. He visited some points of historical interest, such as the Battery and Trinity church, and also Central Park and Wall

Street. His chief attention was given to humanity. "The proper study of mankind is man," some one has said, and so thought he. Some letters of introduction and the good offices of a friend secured him admittance into several well-known circles of *parvenu* society. At a reception given by a princely Cuban gentleman at his residence on Fifth Avenue, the young rustic traveler created something of a sensation by expressions of his frank curiosity and by his awkward but sometimes laughable disregard for the mere formalities of etiquette. When the first of these conventional errors was committed the young ladies of the company had evidently much difficulty in repressing their risibilities and the dude young gentlemen looked contemptuous. Before the entertainment ended the situation changed somewhat. The company discovered that the bashful stranger was easily exasperated into a, to them, novel creature, and before a week had passed after that initiation into the social mysteries of the rich, he had plenty of invitations to all sorts of private parties from well-known society people who seemed to regard him as a sort of *rara avis* and who were outwardly and reputedly highly respectable, and commonly styled "big bugs" by more ordinary and poorer people. During his association among this class of people for a few weeks he was partially dazzled by outward splendor and magnificence. It was a grand sight to his eyes to behold, for the first time, ladies decorated in the most gorgeous style, assembled in elegant drawing rooms or moving through the stately measures of the dance with gentlemen of the most polished manners and courtly bearing, clad scrupulously in full dress suits and overflowing with honey-words. But, alas, how sadly those grand scenes of beauty and grandeur were sometimes marred, when the real nature of many of those jeweled dames, sparkling young ladies and courtly gentlemen was more intimately known!

During young Hemenway's sojourn in New York City, he joined excursions to Albany, Boston and Washington, D. C. The national capital was peculiarly interesting to him because of its importance as the seat of the greatest government on earth, with its public buildings, notable men, foreign embassies and other great public officers. Rutherford B. Hayes was then President of the United States. When Mr. Hemenway was introduced to him at the White House he looked pale, careworn and fagged out. Nevertheless he was very courteous and affable to every one, and his wife seemed especially amiable and desirous to please. The White House was something of a marvel to our young pilgrim, not so much because of its architectural impressiveness as by reason of its associations. It had been the home of the martyred Lincoln and the scenes which had once been consecrated by his presence seemed almost holy ground. Then the Capitol building with its marble statues of the great statesmen and philosophers who in former days had given shape to the genius of the American nation; with its halls where Congress formulates the laws of the land; with its magnificient proportions and solemn grandeur, was an object for much patriotic contemplation and curious observation. Then there were the Patent Office with its appended marvelous collection of models, the War Department and the Treasury Department all redundant with items of interest. There were some relics of George Washington and General Jackson and old battle flags and innumerable articles, valuable chiefly because of their historic associations. But more wonderful than all to the eyes and mind of our traveler were such men as Roscoe Conkling, James G. Blaine, Alexander H. Stephens, who was then alive, and many other famous men whose lives have been largely spent in the public service. From only a casual introduction to these men he learned something of the traits which make men the favorites of the people in this Republic. Their suave address; their keen intellects; their ability to conceal their real thoughts and evade dangerous questions; their uniform will power; their profound feelings and usually lofty spirit were all apparent in their eyes, language and manner on the slightest occasion. It has been said that Conkling is overbearing and haughty, but we did not find him so. To us Blaine was more harsh and repulsive, but Alexander H. Stephens though a cripple and physically incapable of much exertion, struck us as an even higher style of erudite and honest manly intelligence. He was not so dexterous and dashing as either Conkling or the Plumed Knight, but to us he appeared not the less truly great. Our rustic imagination had led us to picture the officers of the nation's government, such as Senators and Representatives, in a very false light. We had thought that a Congressman was something more than a man, and so they sometimes are, perhaps; but a brief stay in Washington satisfied us that they were not demi-gods as we had supposed. Indeed many of them were very ordinary mortals, evidently fond of the good things of life and always keeping a sharp weather eye upon the main chance of winning something more than a vegetable living.

In the course of our stay in the national capital, we met several notorious lobbyists; a few of them were ex-Congressmen; others were attorneys of doubtful character, and one or two were vivacious, cunning women. They all pretended to be the bosom friends of particular Congressmen and were ready to undertake any task from that of securing you an introduction to the British Minister or a clerkship in the Treasury Department, to procuring an immense subsidy for any sort of railway, canal or steamboat enterprise or any other job. Most of this class of creatures could lie with all the earnestness and unction of a superannuated, fashionable deacon that can never prevaricate by virtue of his ecclesiastical office.

CHAPTER III.

Short of Funds.—A Voyage to Rio de Janeiro, Brazil.—Homesickness.—A Hasty Return.—Changed by Experience.—Penniless and Friendless in the Streets of New Orleans.

A FEW months of travel and residence in the chief great cities of the east made sweeping inroads upon Hemenway's purse, and early in 1880 he began to consider how to replenish his depleted exchequer. He returned to New York City early in February and for several days answered the newspaper advertisements of parties desiring clerks, book-keepers, salesmen and the like. After having made a multitude of applications for various positions without success, the agent of a Brazilian coffee plantation offered to send him to Para or Rio Janeiro to serve as a book-keeper on a plantation in the interior. The offer was greedily accepted. It afforded the young adventurer exactly the opportunity he desired—the opportunity to earn something and to visit a foreign land at the same time. Before the first of March he had reached Havana, Cuba; whence he elected to go directly to Rio de Janeiro, the famous capital of the Brizilian empire. The sea voyage was all accomplished on board steamers, and was not remarkable in any particular. Of course the change of climate, the novelty of the southern skies with their particular constellations, and a thousand other things were new and interesting to the young voyager, but they are common to the sight and experience of all who travel from New York to Rio Janeiro and we will not dwell upon them here because they have been described so often by previous travelers. Finally, the harbor of Rio Janeiro was reached one lovely evening, just as the sun was going down, amid a sea of glory, in the west. The custom house officers and a medical examiner came aboard. There was no sickness among either passengers or crew and before morning the good ship was safely anchored near the wharves. It is a picturesque city—this Rio Janeiro is—but young Hemenway had not yet learned how to make his travels most profitable. He landed and roamed about the city, gazing at everything very much as if it was all a menagerie. He gazed at the various notable buildings but without enquiring who occupied them or for what purpose they had been built; he was fascinated by trees with strange foliage and flowers of new kinds but took no trouble to ask their names; yet most of all he gazed in astonishment at the people who were so strange in appearance and spoke such a strange tongue! He had learned something of the Spanish and Portuguese languages from school books, but, alas, he could scarcely understand a word of the ordinary Brizilian colloquial—brogue. That is a wonderful impression which is made upon a young individual when he finds himself for the first time in a foreign land where a totally strange language is spoken by a kind of people never seen before; where the very architecture seems to belong to another world and where the atmosphere, the sun, the stars and the face of nature and humanity all have an unusual, alien aspect.

Eventually young Hemenway found his way to the American minister's residence, and it was a real pleasure to chat with a fellow countryman after having spent a day or so among foreigners. Of the American minister he secured directions how to reach the plantation where he was to work as a bookkeeper. The third day after his arrival in the city he set out by rail—and a rough, primitive railroad it was, too—and after many causeless delays, arrived, some days later, at Tampaco, a small, dirty, inland town, near which the plantation where he thought to pass the next few months of his life was located. Here he met

the manager of the plantation, a big black
Portuguese gentleman who spoke some English.
He had already secured a book-keeper, and maintained that his agent—and partner, as he proved
to be, visiting New York—had no business to
send down a book-keeper. When he found that
nearly a month's salary and fare for passage had
been advanced to Hemenway, as a guarantee of
good faith, he determined that the young American should act as a sort of timekeeper or overseer
of laborers or slaves at low wages until the
advanced money was paid back. This Hemenway refused to do; he would be book-keeper or at
any rate have the sum agreed upon per month,
or he would not work. A quarrel seemed likely
to ensue but somebody called the worthy manager aside and the wrangle was postponed to be
settled on the morrow. But before the next day
dawned Hemenway was well on his way back to
Rio Janeiro where he arrived in due time. A
day or two later he applied to the American consul for employment or assistance to return to the
United States. That functionary would not lend
a helping hand in any way, and Hemenway then
applied to the British consul, who promptly gave
him temporary employment and two weeks later
secured him passage in the capacity of super-

cargo on an English vessel bound for Jamaica. After a long and tedious voyage the ship reached Kingston, and thence Hemenway fortunately secured an immediate passage to Havana. And a few days later he sailed for New Orleans.

Before leaving Rio Janeiro a kind of homesickness seized him; he felt a curious impulse to hurry back to his native land, which entirely eclipsed all desire for adventurous travel; foreign countries were not what they were cracked up to be in histories and narratives of travel, and until he landed in New Orleans he was impatient to hasten back to "the land of the free and the home of the brave." One morning in September, 1880, he shouldered a small valise full of clothes and stepped upon the wharf in New Orleans, with only a dollar and thirty cents in his pocket, after a very brief and barren sojourn in distant Rio. He left New York some seven months before, a callow, inexperienced visionary, overflowing with the most absurd ideas of every description, cherishing an impracticable and Quixotic ambition, with the restlessness, impatience and sentimental enthusiasm of a school-boy. He returned to New Orleans after the lapse of a little less than two-thirds of a year so entirely changed in mind, ambition and personal appearance that his own mother would not have recognized him. He left New York with soft white hands and a slender body clad in the most gentlemanly attire; he returned to New Orleans with sunburned brow, enlarged, thick hands, roughened and calloused by reefing sail in tropical seas, and he was clothed also in the patched and swaggering garb of a dilapidated sailor.

After disembarking once more on the soil of his native land, he wandered about in a brown study, for some time, with all his earthly possessions in a small grip sack in his hand. Finally he reached Canal Street, one of the chief thoroughfares of New Orleans, and being a little tired he seated himself at the base of a pedestal upon which stood the heroic statue of a dead statesman. People passed by him on every side but he observed them not. The great problem of life to the masses confronted him; want stared him in the face; amid wealth and crowds of people he was destitute and alone. What should he do? Where should he go? He had learned something of the practical hardships of life; he had passed through a few of the storms that either break or make a sturdy individuality; he had been under the fire of a tropical sun, under a brutal captain, among brutal men, on the high seas without a sign of land in sight for days and weeks together. He had thrice weathered storms before the mast on shipboard when the angry waves tossed the vessel like a feather in the wind, and the gale screamed through her shrouds, increasing to a dismal hurricane, carrying away everything that was not lashed fast and every moment seeming to threaten her annihilation. Grandly terrific scenes were these! Amid them in the hour of utmost peril he had been happiest! What a peculiar nature! Well, now he was confronted with a new kind of danger. What could he do without money or decent clothes in a great city, among fellow countrymen, indeed, but all indifferent strangers to him? Serious condition!—one that requires, nay, demands some thought, and Hemenway did think about it for three full hours that afternoon, during which time, with his hands against his face and his elbows on his knees, he sat upon the base of a pedestal in the middle of Canal Street, New Orleans, September, 1880—not so very long ago!

CHAPTER IV.

Not every Man that cares to practice his own Philosophy.—
Adventures in New Orleans.

ALLUDING to the career of Benjamin Disraeli, the Earl of Beaconsfield, an English Jew who broke the ban against his class, and, after many defeats and failures, raised himself to the highest station of honor and power which any British subject can attain, some anonymous poet has said:

> He grappled with his evil star;
> He broke his birth's invidious bar;
> Reversed the luckless turns of chance,
> And fought untoward circumstance:
> He wrung from an attainted fate
> The highest rank subjects can take,
> And blazoned on the scroll of fame
> His hated, foreign, Jewish name.

Many interesting facts have been adduced from the lives of eminent men to prove that genuine worth and merit are stimulated in their development by hereditary disadvantages, by poverty and misfortune. It has also been argued, but not so successfully, that a republican form of government, like that of the United States, affords talent and genius the best opportunity for successful development. Perhaps this is in a measure true, but it is also indisputably a fact that where the will, determination and innate ability of the individual are not wanting, disadvantage of birth, the interdictions of discriminating laws and conventional systems, poverty and obscurity and adversity are only the spurs which excite the ardor of ambition into irresistible momentum, even as the coquettish, and sometimes cruel repulses of a modest maiden only intensify the affection and zeal of her favored lover, until his devotion breaks over every barrier and wins the prize. It is true that dire misfortunes and disadvantages do not stimulate inferior people, but if such things fail to arouse a man, albeit to apparently superhuman exertion, nothing can make him either successful or great. On the other hand inherited wealth and hereditary power would tempt the majority of men to indulge idleness, despotism or dissipation. The prize looses half its charm when it is won without a struggle. In a manner very similar to this would juvenile Charles W. Hemenway have theorized prior to the day when he left home where he had always enjoyed every comfort whether he had earned it or not. A little later, after he had begun his career as a traveler, we have seen how disappointment in Brazil was followed by an abnormal sentimental desire to return to his native land. Although he had not sufficient means to pay all of the passage fare, his return was facilitated by a favorable although a rough fortune, and then he was left virtually penniless and almost in rags to reap the benefits of poverty according to his vaunted theory that want and distress ought to stimulate the growth and development of strength and wisdom in character. Well, it is not every man that cares to practice his favorite philosophy. Young Hemenway had done so; he had deliberately cut himself loose from the shelter of a father's roof, from the protection of true and tried friends and pushed the yet fragile bark of his destiny out into mid ocean; he had basked in sunshine awhile, and then weathered hard gales and then he found himself in New Orleans in a condition very much the same as if he had been shipwrecked upon a rock. We left him in the last chapter brooding over his situation silently in the streets. There he sat absorbed in meditation until the declining sun began to herald the approach of night. Then suddenly he started up as if he had all at once remembered something that he must attend to forthwith. He had gone but a few paces when he met a well-dressed gentleman of whom he politely enquired the name and location of the best hotel in the city.

"Well, Jack," answered the stranger, "what in h—l do you want of a hotel; go back to your hammock in the fo'castle; you must be drunk."

"Sir," rejoined Hemenway, "I have no hammock to go to and I am not drunk; I asked you a decent question civilly and if you were a gentleman you would frankly and courteously reply."

"Who are you?" demanded the stranger, with an awkward stare.

"I am a man just arrived from Brazil, and only enquiring of you the name and location of the best hotel in the city," was the reply.

The stranger suddenly changed his tone and blandly designated the St. Charles Hotel, on a street by the same name, near by, in response to Hemenway's enquiries. The latter thanked his informant and proceeded forthwith to the St. Charles Hotel, which was a rather stately and massive large, stone structure and undoubtedly the best public house in New Orleans. The advent of a dilapidated sailor, with an old grip sack under his arm, created not a little surprise in the hotel office, but when Hemenway applied to the clerk for a room in a sober voice, astonishment took the place of surprise. After the clerk recovered himself he rather politely stated that strangers without baggage must pay in advance. Hemenway demanded the price for one night's lodging, and the clerk demanded two dollars. This was more money than the would-be guest could muster, and he didn't believe that was the regular rate. Just then he noticed a card in a daily paper on the counter advertising elegant rooms with board for $7.00 per week. It flashed across his mind that the hotel clerk was trying to tax him double price, and that functionary manifested a desire to have him march on.

"See here," said Hemenway, at a venture, "I will pay you no more than regular rates: give me a room," and he planked down a dollar.

The clerk paused a moment; said not a word except to whisper to a porter who presently beckoned Hemenway to follow him. To a small apartment near the servants' quarters the guest was conducted, where he arranged his toilet somewhat, exchanged his coarse sailor's trousers for a very good pair of black pantaloons from his bag, a vest from the same source was also put on, and then he went out and got shaved. After that he went into the first hat store that he came to and asked credit for a hat. The proprietor did a strictly cash business, of course the salesman said. Hemenway enquired for the proprietor. That gentleman was in a neat little private office; he was just preparing to go home. Hemenway asked for credit for not only a hat but a coat also, with the air of a man who expected to have his request granted, and before the good-natured merchant replied, Hemenway began a small oration which the merchant frequently interrupted with curious queries. In the end Hemenway got the goods and put them on. The coat and hat selected were of fine quality and were priced at $16.00. Hemenway offered to give his note for that amount payable in thirty days, although he had not the slightest idea where the money would come from, and only felt such reliance upon his own ability that he was confident he could meet the obligation. However, the merchant evidently thought that a note would be no good if he was dealing with a rogue, and that if his creditor was honest he would get his pay anyway, and declined to be troubled with a note. Indeed, he said, he would not even charge up the bill, but trust entirely to his strange customer's honor for payment.

Young Hemenway tried to make a similar arrangement with another dealer for a pair of fine shoes and some white underclothes. At first, and even at three different establishments, he failed in this undertaking, but at a fourth store he succeeded in obtaining a pair of shoes and three white shirts, some collars, a necktie and a pair of socks on credit.

Anyone who knows how next to impossible it is for an unaccredited stranger, in shabby garments, especially, and with no reference as to character and the like, to obtain the least thing on credit of merchants in large cities, will appreciate how great a difficulty Hemenway had surmounted when he obtained his new clothes in this case. He was not a member of any secret society, had not a friend or acquaintance in all New Orleans, and his only capital was a fluent tongue which told briefly and frankly all about himself, his condition and his aspirations.

Equipped with neat apparel, Hemenway returned to the hotel and dressed up. It was after ten o'clock in the evening when he got on his new toggery and he had not tasted food since morning. With twenty cents in his pocket and a feeling of the utmost peace and confidence, he sought out a restaurant and paid fifteen cents for a cup of coffee and some bread. A little later, with only five cents to his name, he went to bed and was soon sound asleep.

CHAPTER V.

Struggling with Fortune.—A lucky Sale of Manuscript.— Trusting to the Promptings of an inner Monitor.

IN the eyes of most people, good clothes and a dignified deportment are the essential items in the composition of a lady or a gentleman the world over. Thoughtful minds which rise above the common-place level of the masses may differ with this view and be correct, but nevertheless we must pay due defference to the opinions and prejudices of the majority be they right or wrong. If a man would associate with people of wealth, influence, social standing and ability, he must at least be externally fit to be seen in their company.

When Hemenway made his appearance before the office desk of the St. Charles Hotel the morning after his arrival, clothed in very presentable style, there was a very perceptible change in the manner of the clerk, who, without asking pay in advance, politely suggested that breakfast was waiting—and this serves to illustrate the popular effect of clothes.

Half an hour later Hemenway might have been seen leaving the St. Charles Hotel with a small parcel under his arm. It contained a large variety of original manuscript compositions and a diary written by the young traveler during his long passage from Rio Janeiro to New Orleans. In all there were some two or three hundred pages of this manuscript, which was very legible but in no shape for publication except in small detached portions which might have been suitable for newspaper articles. The young man was in hopes that he might be able to dispose of this manuscript for a few dollars, and with the purpose of negotiating its sale he visited several newspaper offices in vain. Editors generally had no time to struggle through over two hundred closely written pages of composition upon a multitude of subjects, but finally the writer became so persistent, that a reporter of the *Picayune* was detailed to "look the stuff over." The reporter evidently did not relish the job, and he recommended the author to offer the manuscript to a literary gentleman who lived in Camp Street.

Hemenway in despair followed the reporter's advice. The gentleman referred to was a middle-aged, high-toned person. He was not a permanent resident of New Orleans. His name was Henry A. Jarvis. In conversation he was artificial and high-strung. The scribe informed him at great length about the circumstances under which the manuscript was written; about the contents and about the writer's pressing necessities for a little cash. Mr. Jarvis was visibly affected; he would do anything to aid a struggling young "man of letters;" he would look the manuscript over and pay all it was worth. In the meantime he would see that the writer got a living, and, acting upon this word of promise, he advanced ten dollars. Hemenway put the money in his pocket with a feeling of relief and joy that cannot be described. It was nearly four o'clock in the afternoon. He almost ran back to the hotel and paid his bill. Then he gathered up his effects and started off to find a private residence where boarders were taken. He soon secured a furnished apartment on St. Charles Street. The rent paid in advance was only three dollars per week. Meals were secured at a restaurant.

The next day Hemenway started out in search of employment. He hardly thought that Mr.

Jarvis would be likely to pay any more for the manuscript. He visited any number of stores of all sorts, and everywhere expressed himself as ready to do anything that was honorable and legitimate to make a living. He also stopped a large number of men as he met them on the street and urged his claims for employment. One of the men, thus incidentally applied to, was a brewer, and he offered the writer a place in a grog shop, but the offer was declined with thanks. Finally a drayman was found who wanted a man to drive a team; wages $35.00 per month and board. That was honest business, and it was accepted. He began the dray business at once, and followed the calling of a driver for at least three days, and he still retains a certificate of his employer stating that he "was the best hand" the said employer ever had. On the evening of the third day after beginning the new business of driving a dray, he chanced to pass near the post office and stopped to enquire at the general delivery for mail. There was a letter for him from Henry A. Jarvis, requesting him to call at once at that gentleman's abode. In compliance with this request, later in the evening, he visited that gentleman, who received him very kindly and at once began to talk business. He would pay liberally for the manuscript providing Hemenway would in writing relinquish all right and title to the same. "All right," said Hemenway. "I will give you $260.00 if you will sign this bill of sale," put in Jarvis. "All right," was the reply again; and forthwith the author put his signature to the paper without reading it. Jarvis noticed this and took the trouble to read the document aloud. It was merely an agreement by which all right and title to said manuscript was transferred by the author to Mr. Jarvis, "to use and dispose of as he chose."

Mr. Jarvis paid cash down; he even refused to deduct the $10.00 which he had advanced from the total amount that he agreed to pay, and the young man took his departure from the presence of his customer without more ado. When he got out into the street it was with difficulty that he kept from pulling off his hat and yelling at the top of his voice for joy; he danced down the sidewalk in such an unceremonious fashion that a police officer and a number of ladies began to stare in a way that made him a little less demonstrative. Two hundred and sixty dollars! Good gracious! He had often been in possession of several times that amount, but this two hundred and sixty dollars just then seemed to be the biggest sum he ever heard of. If he had suddenly discovered a gold mine or struck a flowing oil well, he could not have felt more entirely surprised or elated. He could not be certain whether Mr. Jarvis had really considered the manuscript worth what he paid for it, or whether he was a rich man who desired to be generous, merely. And so he did not know whether to consider himself a good writer or a subject of eleemosynary aid; though, to be frank about it, he was inclined to think he had made a clever hit with his pen. The very evening that he received the unexpected money for his manuscript, he paid his debts, to the surprise of his only creditors who had trusted him for clothes, and to the infinite satisfaction of himself. When he had contracted these debts he had no idea where the money to pay them was coming from, but somehow, he felt they would be paid. In those days he was not religious; he had become disgusted with the regulation Christian creeds of his acquaintance, and the doings of Christians and their manifestly false doctrines had made him almost doubt the existence of the God of the Bible, but still he believed in an overruling Providence who would help those who helped themselves; and he also trusted to the promptings of an inner monitor which he was accustomed to speak of as the "spirit of his lucky star." When he was in the extremity of difficulty or perplexity, and earnestly sought to know what course to pursue, that "spirit" never failed to offer its subtle suggestions, which, in turn, had proved *always* for the best.

CHAPTER VI.

Where General Jackson Whipped the British.—Colonel Varres.—Again at Sea.—Conjugal Infidelity and Murder.

WITH his debts paid, a handsome little sum of money in his pocket, and very good clothes, Hemenway did not deem himself constrained to work at the drayage business any longer, and he resigned his position on the truck to look for a more paying occupation. The last days of September, 1880, were now near at hand. New Orleans was showing signs of an approaching unhealthful season. It became desirable to leave the quaint old environs of the city. The young adventurer paid a visit to the scene of the battle of New Orleans, where General Jackson whipped the British during or after the close of the war of 1812. He also visited other scenes made memorable in history by General Benjamin F. Butler during the Rebellion. The city of New Orleans itself is peculiarly interesting to one born and reared at the north. It has a mixed population consisting of negroes, half-breeds, Creoles, descendants of the French, and half-breed Americans. To all intents and purposes it is also a seaport city; for the broad waters of the Mississippi, not far away, flow into the Gulf of Mexico, furnishing a deep and safe channel for the largest seafaring vessels.

While Hemenway was seeking acceptable employment, he traveled through every section of the place, and took especial delight in studying human nature as it was there manifested. In the course of his peregrinations he made the acquaintance of Colonel Don Varres who claimed to be a Mexican by birth, and a pure blooded Spaniard by descent. The Colonel soon learned that Hemenway was in search of employment, and after enquiring something of the young man's history, he engaged the youth at a very munificent salary. It did not appear very clear as to the nature of the business in which Colonel Varres was engaged, but he claimed that he owned a number of vessels engaged in the transportation of different commodities along the coast of Texas, and between the ports of Texas and Mexico. He wanted a trustworthy man to look after different cargoes; to superintend the exchange of exported articles with retail dealers along the coast of Mexico and Yucatan. In consideration of a monthly salary of $400, Hemenway eagerly accepted the position. He at once entered the Colonel's service and aided him in making a number of wholesale purchases. About the first of October, Varres and his new employe started for Galveston where the Colonel's goods were transferred to boats and shipped for the mouth of the Rio Grande River or some intervening port. Without delay, in company with several Mexicans, Varres and his new servant set out by stage over a circuitous route for Corpus Christi. The party at length reached a point on the coast not far from Corpus Christi, and late one pleasant, peaceful evening, a large brig appeared a league or so off shore, with which signals were exchanged. A little later a boat from the brig touched the shore, and Colonel Varres and Hemenway, with two Mexicans, were taken off to the vessel, which immediately spread her canvas and ran before a moderate breeze for the southeast. Before the sun arose, land had disappeared from view. On board the vessel there was nothing very unusual in appearance. The brig was capable of carrying a vast amount of sail, though, and she was also of comparatively light draft, and evidently built with a view to some speed. She was only partly loaded with a miscellaneous cargo of calicoes, Yankee notions, and dry goods. She was manned by a Mexican half-breed crew, and Varres himself acted as captain. His wife and two little daughters occupied the cabin. There were no passengers on board. Donna Varres was a young and singularly tall Spanish woman, with large, deep black eyes, and long, jet black hair. Her two daughters were mere children, the oldest being not over six or seven years. When Colonel Varres first boarded the vessel, the little children ran and kissed him, but the mother remained in the cabin, and when, after some delay, her husband entered, many loud and angry words passed between them, which were readily heard by the sailors in their quarters. Though recently accustomed to life at sea, Hemenway was quite seasick during the forenoon, and he stretched himself upon a huge mat under an awning on the top of the cabin. It had been understood that Vera Cruz was the destination of the vessel, but that she might sail from there further south, before discharging her cargo. Anyone who has been seasick will understand with what apathy Hemenway passed the first few hours on board the brig. Although the sky was clear, the Gulf was rough, and a strong breeze was blowing. Towards noon the vessel changed her course and sailed west by south. At two o'clock the wind stiffened into a light gale and sail had to be taken in, but before sundown the wind moderated again, and the sailors spread every available yard of canvas. Varres had spent most of the day on deck. Only once had he gone below. He kept the sailors busy mending old sail and painting the vessel. As the sun was about to go down in splendor beneath the western horizon, the Colonel summoned Hemenway to dinner, and at the same time informed him that he would leave the brig in Hemenway's charge during the first watch of the night. Then Varres entered the cabin and Hemenway was about to follow, when the Colonel came struggling back on deck, muttering incoherently; from his back and side the blood was streaming. He staggered forward a few feet and then fell heavily. The sailors rushed to his side and raised him to convey him below. He moved not a muscle; he said not a word. Upon the cabin table they laid his body. The first mate felt of his pulse; the medicine chest was opened and restoratives administered, and repeated efforts were made to stop the flow of blood which was still oozing in an irregular stream from a large red gash in the back—but all in vain; Varres was dead. But where was his widow? Where was she who in life or death should have been by his side? With her daughters she had locked herself in the Colonel's room and firmly refused to speak, until a sailor began to batter the door down, when in wild accents she threatened to shoot the first individual that attempted to force his way in. That woman was a murderess; it was her hand that had driven the fatal blade into her own husband's side. Why had she committed such a bloody deed? She said it was because she had discovered that husband's conjugal infidelity. Such a tragedy is bad enough and shocking enough on land, but it is a thousand times more terrible on shipboard, away out at sea. It was getting dark; the vessel's lights were not yet displayed; the sailors were grouped around the stiffening corpse, and only the man at the wheel was at his post. Some one must take command or serious consequences might ensue, for again the wind began to blow almost a gale. Hemenway had been almost stupefied, but he was aroused now. The sailors were ordered to reef sail; they obeyed, and when the vessel was stripped of much of her canvas, the sailors were recalled to prepare for the dead captain's burial. In that climate a corpse cannot be kept long. The mournful task was performed carefully and tenderly by the rude tars. They had evidently loved their dead master, and many a tear welled from their eyes and trickled down their weather-stained cheeks as they wrapped the body in the sails that were to be its coffin. Finally when this sad labor had been performed, the remains were deposited in the hold of the vessel, and a guard placed over them. During the night the murderess emerged from her place of refuge. The sailors seized and placed her in irons. She shed some tears, but was sullenly mute when questioned. The hours of the night passed on; the sailors moved about silently like black spectres; the brig flew on before a stiff breeze which later quickened into a heavy gale, and howled a dismal requiem through the shrouds, while the sea lashed herself into fury as if enraged by the blood that had been spilled upon her bosom but a few hours before. That was a scene, impressive and dreadful in the extreme! Not a soul on board slept all night long.

Hemenway paced the deck until the grey dawn of morning; and to him the recollection of that night is like the horrid remembrance of an awful nightmare.

CHAPTER VII.

Forebodings.—Shipwrecked.—Coffined among Shells and Sharks.

DARING and venturesome nature may enjoy a storm at sea as long as the vessel springs no leak and floats far from rocks and breakers. There is a kind of awful sublimity in the aspect of the raging waves torn into spray by the fierce gale; and then a ship tossed about like a feather, but defying sea and storm, affords some men a temporary habitation which is to them at once a peril and a delight. But when the gale stiffens into a hurricane; when the masts snap, and the hull springs a leak, and the vessel ships water and ceases to respond to the rudder; when no land is in sight and the raging sea is desolate of a single sail, the mariner discards all possibly pleasurable interest in the contending elements, and only looks forward to the approaching horrible certainty of shipwreck and perhaps a watery grave, preceded, it may be, by untold hardships or starvation.

When Hemenway was riding through the night towards the Gulf shore, to embark on board the brig, which rejoiced in the name of the *Donna Garcia,* and which at this stage of his history was bearing him with the corpse of his whilom master to an unknown destiny, he had felt a singular ominous dread come over the spirit of bright anticipations, which the prospect of a voyage in a new quarter and $400 per month naturally inspired. But his old fondness of adventure came back and then also for the first time he discovered that he had acquired a love for money. In his pocket he carried over $500 in gold—a month's salary advanced and what he had saved from the proceeds of his manuscript. When the spirit of foreboding dread passed over his soul he had but to place his hand upon the coin, and all doubtful feeling vanished as by enchantment. A little later the shocking assassination of his master stunned and horrified him, and before many hours had passed he began to realize that his future was again as uncertain as the wind.

It was hardly six o'clock the morning after the

murder, and the second day of the voyage, when Hemenway, who had assumed command of the vessel, summoned the mate for a consultation. Evidently the mate had been a trusted confident of the late captain and proprietor, but could furnish little or no information as to the condition of the dead man's estates, or as to the whereabouts of his nearest relatives. During the night the mate had kept the brig upon her southern course as nearly as the sometimes contrary winds would permit, and he suggested that it would be well to consult the wife-murderess as to the intentions of her late husband. This suggestion was immediately acted upon. The two men proceeded to the fo'castle, where the murderess was then confined. Her two little daughters were with her, and she presented a pitiful picture, indeed. She had evidently not slept during the night, and was weeping bitterly. When first addressed she refused to speak, but a few kind words induced her to unbosom herself freely. She first enquired what was to be done with her. When informed that nothing had yet been determined upon, she seemed relieved. She said her late husband had no home except his ship. Again she repeated the story of his conjugal infidelity, and justified her bloody deed. She pleaded that she might be thrown overboard, rather than be taken ashore and turned over to legal authorities in the United States, and then she begged for the sake of her children that she might be spared and landed in Mexico. While the interview was still in progress, one of the sailors came in great haste to the mate and summoned the men on deck. For several hours a strong gale had been blowing, and now directly to the windward of the vessel, and apparently but a few leagues distant, a great baloon-shaped, black cloud was visible. The mate pronounced it a "black squall," and perhaps it might have been more properly called a tornado. In tones of thunder the mate ordered every man on deck. With all possible haste everything on board was secured, the hatches closed, and everything made fast for the anticipated storm, but although the sailors struggled away as if their lives depended upon their exertions, the last sail had not been made fast to the spars when a terrific blast struck the vessel. For an instant she seemed to quiver like a reed and the next moment she reeled upon her beam ends and then careened over. Before she righted herself a monster wave swept her decks and she seemed entirely submerged for a time. Hemenway was standing by the wheel when the storm struck the brig, and he managed to maintain his hold upon a chain secured around the cabin. When the vessel came out of the first shock, her main mast was in splinters and every spar was gone or hanging by the rigging. Four sailors had been washed overboard and left no trace of their doom in the foaming sea. The rest of the crew, with the mate, soon severed the hanging spars and the wreck of the mainmast which still hung to the vessel and threatened to swamp her. For nearly an hour the storm continued to rage with unabated fury. The waters of the Gulf foamed and seethed like a raging torrent. The mighty waves arose in huge walls of liquid destruction, ever and anon sweeping completely over the dismantled vessel which now seemed lifted to the heavens and then appeared sunk down as into the valley of the shadow of death. When at last the wind became a trifle less boisterous and the sky a little less black, it was discovered that the unmanageable wreck was leaking badly. All hands were put to work on the pumps for a while and then it was deemed advisable to throw a part of the cargo overboard. Many bales of merchandise were cast into the sea but with little or no effect. The dismantled hulk was filling with water, and it was evident that the time was not far distant when she must be abandoned or go down with all on board. The wind continued to abate and the sea became a little less angry. But still the water in the hold kept creeping up, inch by inch, in spite of the most desperate efforts to check its progress. At this time there were on board, all told, some nine souls, namely: four sailors, Hemenway, the mate, the dead Captain's widow and her two daughters. All were assembled in the partly wrecked cabin to hold a consultation.

What was to be done? Ah! it is such a condition that levels all mankind—that makes them all equal and all humble and adjusts all differences of opinion, creed or color. No one was even disposed to reproach the murderess now. For the last four or five hours she had labored like a common seaman to save the brig. Twice she had narrowly escaped being washed overboard, but still she labored on, first at the pumps, then in the hold, helping to discharge a part of the cargo, and finally she assisted in repairing the vessel's damaged boats. Immediately after the great storm struck the brig, the brave woman demanded to be released from her chains. Then she had firmly lashed her daughters to the stump of the mainmast and went to work with a hatchet to cut loose the debris still hanging by the rigging. Her courage and daring was almost astonishing and she looked like some uncanny spirit as she moved about, ax in hand, her long hair hanging in wild disorder, and her whole person dripping wet with water, which every now and then swept in violent waves over the ill-fated vessel.

After a long and serious discussion, a lunch with brandy was served to all on board, and after some further examination of the hull, which appeared to be leaking more and more as the hours passed on, a unanimous agreement to abandon the wreck and take to the boats was reached. There were three small boats left; there had been five but two had been smashed by the water. These three boats had been badly damaged and one of them would leak still, although every effort had been made to repair it. It was believed that the Texas coast might be easily reached in a few days, even in these open frail structures, providing the weather would only moderate, and at the same time it was deemed unsafe to remain over night on board the wreck. When this decision was reached, the brig's chronometer indicated that it was after four o'clock p. m., but all hands went to work with a will. Several casks were filled with fresh water; provisions were carefully packed; a compass for each boat was found; some spare canvas was taken from the mate's quarters; all the gold and silver on board—and there were several thousand dollars—were secured; some knives, fish hooks, canned meats and vegetables, with other miscellaneous articles, were got in readiness to be transferred to the boats. By this time the wind had begun to die out entirely although the Gulf was very rough. However, it was not yet dark and the boats were lowered fortunately without any accident. In a short time everything necessary had been transferred to them and the sailors pulled clear of the wreck, but none too soon; for hardly half an hour later in the gray twilight the *Donna Garcia* reeled up on end and went down in plain view of the shipwrecked crew, carrying with her the cold body of her owner and captain to be coffined among the shells and sharks and mermaids of the deep.

CHAPTER VIII.

Adrift in Open Boats.—Dashed upon the Sand.—Through Mexico.—Señor Luna's Family.

THE three boats kept within sight of each other until dark. The waters of the Gulf became less boisterous, but still there was constant danger of capsizing. The best of the boats was occupied by Mrs. Varres, her two children, the mate and one able-bodied seaman. The other two boats were smaller, and two men occupied each one. All had agreed to keep the same general direction as near as possible, and steered for the north. In the boat which Hemenway occupied there were ample provisions to last two men a week. His companion was a huge Mexican half-breed who spoke and understood little or no English. By turns the two men tugged at the oars and sat at the helm during the night. When morning came the sea was so calm that both men decided to rest, and after partaking of an ample meal, both lay down in the bottom of the boat and were soon fast asleep. It was long after midday before either of them awoke. Hemenway was the first to open his eyes. The weather was still fair. After another lunch, they both took hold of the oars and pulled until after dark. The second night was passed much as the first had been. Again the day was devoted to rest, and the third and fourth nights passed uneventfully. The other boats had not been seen since the night the wreck was deserted. On the morning of the fourth day evidences of land were visible, but a baffling wind set in during the afternoon, and before dark the water was very rough, and navigation in such a small craft was hazardous and difficult in the extreme. However, the wind shifted into a more favorable quarter, and the prospect of reaching land the next day was encouraging. Clouds obscured the sky, but after midnight the weather again moderated a little. The two men were very nearly exhausted with the toils which they had undergone, and paid little attention to anything except to keep the boat from capsizing. Suddenly, about two o'clock on the fifth night, a rough shock startled the two occupants of the craft. They had scarcely time to look about them when a second and third shock followed, and the water rushed in through a great hole that had been smashed through the bottom of the little boat. There was scarcely a moment for thought. The boat was going to pieces. Hemenway divested himself of his boots and coat, seized an oar, and plunged out into the breakers. It was too dark to see far, and therefore impossible to tell whether the shore was near at hand or not. The first wave landed him high and dry upon a rock and severely stunned him; a second and a third almost lifted him from the foothold he had found. A momentary lull followed, and then wave after wave splashed over him, but he succeeded in obtaining a firm hold upon a jutting edge of the rock whereon he sat, and there he held fast until day began to dawn, when the dim outline of the shore was visible only a few rods off. Gathering up his courage, and convinced that he could not maintain his position much longer, he made for the beach on the crest of a breaker which carried him along with a terrifying velocity, and suddenly dropped him more dead than alive upon the sand, where he laid for several hours in a half-conscious condition. When he revived enough to walk about he found the wreck of the boat, in which he had been cast away, not far off upon the sand, together with the half-filled fresh water cask and some half-spoiled provisions, upon which he feasted. A lunch refreshed and invigorated him. The body of the sailor who had been cast upon the shore with him was also found, but it was bruised, stiff and inanimate. After dragging the remains back from the water and covering them with grass, Hemenway walked along the beach for several miles. He found himself upon the narrow, low strip of land known as Padre Island. Crossing this island near the southern extremity thereof, he hailed a small vessel, and was eventually landed on the mainland of Texas, near the mouth of the Rio Grande River, whence he proceeded to Brownsville, and there rested for a week or so. He had been badly bruised and was almost exhausted, but, thank good fortune! he had carried his gold safely through with him. Scarcely had his wounds healed when he set out for the city of Mexico, traveling day and night, part of the way on horseback, but mainly by stage. At Monterey, in the State of Nuevo Leon, he gave up the notion of visiting the Mexican capital and proceeded to Chihuahua, the capital of a state of the same name. It was a long and dreary ride of nearly or quite six hundred miles, for there were then no railroads in that section of Mexico. With its mixed inhabitants, adobe houses, peculiar and picturesque landscapes, with its air of repose, and the prevailing primitive condition of its civilization, the land of Mexico presented a striking appearance to our young traveler. He had learned enough of the Spanish language to make himself partially understood, and with an eye to the business of seeing the sights and novelties which the country afforded, he nevertheless traveled very much like an amateur excursionist, missing a great deal, if not all, that he should have most desired to observe and study. It must have been about the last of November when he reached Chihuahua, where he determined to stay for a few days, to rest and prepare for a journey to Guaymas on the Gulf of California. At that time (1880) there was no railway in Chihuahua. The spirit of modern progress had not yet invaded its slumbering precincts. It presented that appearance which is typical of all Mexican cities. Although it contained a population of at least ten or twelve thousand souls, there was but one real public house or hotel in the entire place, but in lieu thereof furnished rooms could be readily obtained at a very low rental, and restaurants, such as they were, could be patronized by the traveler, providing he was hungry, and therefore not very particular about the cuisine. Adobe buildings, one story high, were used for residences, shops, stores, and every other purpose. Then, of course, there was the grand plaza where every loafer and beggar in the city loved to congregate, and where more respectable people often assembled to gossip and loiter. From Chihuahua young Hemenway wrote a voluminous account of his travels in Mexico, which was afterwards published in detached sketches in different Chicago and St. Louis papers. From this source his purse was partially replenished. In company with a young Mexican, who boasted an unbroken line of Castilian ancestry, reaching back to the time of the Spanish conquest, Hemenway visited several leading families, merchants, officers and Catholic priests. These people represented the better class of society; they were courteous in the extreme, and particularly hospitable and generous, as well as generally intelligent and well-informed. But no one could fail to note that the masses of the people were inferior, ignorant, and correspondingly degraded. A German-American merchant who had been located in Chihuahua for years, is authority for the statement that vice and degradation in every form were no strangers to the place. He said it was no uncommon thing for lower-class mothers to sell the virtue of their own ten and twelve year old daughters. Shiftlessness, inertia, the dread of labor, were characteristics of the masses.

But it was different with the better classes. We gained admittance to the household of Señor Luna. He was a gentleman of some wealth and possessed a large adobe residence elegantly furnished throughout. The house was built in the form of a hollow square. Suits of rooms extended all around an open court, where an abundance of flowers and plants were grown. Hardly any two of the rooms connected directly with each other. All had doors and windows opening into the court. Señor Luna was a tall and graceful elderly man, with a high forehead, black hair and eyes, and a dignified and courteous manner. He spoke some English. His family consisted of a wife and three daughters; also one or two sons who were absent at school. Señora Luna was seldom seen, and the daughters never received admirers alone or went out in company with young men. In the presence of their father they were shy, modest and reticent. They were slender in form and graceful in movement, their eyes jet black, their hair long and equally dark. Short in stature and prematurely developed into womanhood, they were probably typical Mexican beauties. Servants waited upon them and they lived a life of ease, almost as closely guarded as the inmates of a Turkish harem. They possessed none of the vivacity and were allowed none of the liberty of the American girl. Although tasteful dancers and masters of the guitar and capable of singing Mexican ditties with grace and peculiar pathos, their accomplishments were limited in the extreme, and they seemed only ambitious of becoming the playthings of some gallant man. Their mother had probably been as beautiful as her daughters, once, and as slender and delicate, but now she was fat and "squatty" in appearance and anything but lithe, graceful or attractive. Señor Luna's family was a fair sample of the better class of Mexicans. Religiously, they were devout Catholics. In society and everywhere they were proud, haughty, reserved, rarely gay, never boisterous or hilarious, but always dignified and courteous.

CHAPTER IX.

To Guaymas.—In a Pest-house.—Saved by Sisters of Charity.—To San Francisco and Australia.—A Horrible Scene.

FROM Chihuahua, Hemenway proceeded overland to Guaymas, a considerable Mexican city on the Gulf of California. At the present time there is a railroad connecting Guaymas with El Paso del Norte, and there forming a junction with other railways leading through the United States on the north, and through Chihuahua to the City of Mexico on the south, but in 1880 those railway connections had not been completed, and Guaymas was a dull and comparatively isolated city, enjoying some commercial advantages by virtue of its seaport but otherwise of little consequence notwithstanding its considerable size. The trip overland from Chihuahua to Guaymas in 1880 was interesting in the extreme to a young man fond of exploring regions new to him, and Mr. Hemenway still retains vivid recollections of his emotions while riding by day and night through strange mountain scenery, over barren tracts that will yet be fertilized by the industrial arts of man; through gorges and cañons, where mounds of stones, with a wooden cross, occasionally indicated the spot where reposed the remains of some unfortunate traveler who had been waylaid by Indians or murdered by highwaymen. Then there were occasional Mexican settlements with their dusky inhabitants, full of mystery to the eyes of the young traveler, together with pleasant daily adventures that gave flavor to the monotony of the trip. At one time a great rattlesnake attracted the driver's attention, as it lay asleep in the road, and the sport of killing it was fascinating because of the danger incurred. Again a herd of antelope would pass too near the diligence or stage, and a careful shot now and then brought one of them to the ground. Then there were coyotes to shoot at and an occasional prairie dog town with its strange inhabitants, consisting of prairie dogs, owls and snakes, which seemed to dwell together in harmony.

At Guaymas, young Hemenway was taken sick; the doctors thought he had the yellow fever; he was hustled off to a quarantine hospital, and a few days later dragged out into a sort of dead-house where he lay for a day or so without food or medical attendance. It was a deplorable condition to be in. Alone among strangers, and unable, from sheer weakness, to move enough to turn over, it seemed as if nothing could save him from the grave, but a kindly Providence intervened. Some Sisters of Charity visited the pest-house, and, finding the young man still alive, they moved him into a better apartment, and gave him medicine and food, and nursed him with all the tenderness of a mother. They used to kneel beside his cot and devoutly say their prayers as they counted their beads, and occasionally allowed the tears to stream down their white faces. Once convalescent, the patient speedily recovered. Then without delay he proceeded to San Francisco by steamer. It was about the middle of February, 1881, when he passed through the Golden Gate for the first time. In the metropolis of the west, he remained but a short time. During all his travels he had performed arduous literary labor for different newspapers and magazines, and earned enough money to pay a greater part of his expenses. In California he was fortunate in obtaining the favor of Charles Wilcott Brooks, a man of much literary experience and ability, who secured him many privileges in the way of free passes, and also introduced him to many leaders of society. Hemenway paid visits to San José, Los Angeles, Sacramento and intermediate points of interest. He also visited Angel Island, and, through the courtesy of General McDowell, was kindly received and entertained by officers at the military posts of Angel Island, Alcatraz and The Presidio. He also visited Saucelito, and took particular delight in sailing over San Francisco bay. The weather was occasionally chilly and wet, but at midday it was often pleasant and even warm. Some of the scenery which enfilades the bay is beautiful and even grand, and had a sort of rustic enchantment for the young traveler.

It was near the last of March when Hemenway projected a trip to Australia. After a little delay he finally sailed once more through the Golden Gate, this time outward bound. Thirty days later, after a voyage of some eight or ten thousand miles, he again disembarked from his steamer in the city of Sydney, New South Wales. Port Jackson, the bay upon which Sydney is located, affords a safe harbor to the ships of all nations. The city is nearly, if not quite, as large as San Francisco, and possesses many commercial attractions. The people are mostly English and extremely enterprising. Owing to his ignorance of the country, young Hemenway found himself at quite a disadvantage in his new field of adventure. The climate of the region where Sydney is located is agreeable most parts of the year. The coldest month is July, and the warmest season occurs in January and February. In the main the weather is mild, though sometimes extremely warm, yet rarely, if ever, cold enough to freeze.

Hemenway remained in Australia about a year. Soon after his advent in Sydney his supply of cash was exhausted, and he was reduced to the utmost necessity of exertion. During the following months he passed through a series of trials and vicissitudes that would have crushed a less determined soul. At one time he found himself toiling to perform the duties of a common laborer in the mines of Victoria; at another time he tried the business of driving a stage; again he became a sheep herder for a few weeks, and then a road builder, a sailor, and a miner again in succession. Eventually, after many failures, fortune again smiled upon him; he became a reporter, beginning by furnishing police items, and ending as a writer of especial articles, for which he was handsomely paid. He kept a sort of diary during the latter portion of his stay in Australia. Originally it was his intention to publish the substance of that memorandum in this work, but a desire to give Utah, the "Mormon" question, and the Sandwich Islands some notice in this volume, has persuaded him to reserve the full narrative of his experience in Australia for a future publication. Therefore this portion of his pilgrimage will be chiefly left to occupy the leisure hours of another day—perhaps the latter portion of his present term of imprisonment—when dreary hours may suggest further recourse to the pen for relief from the tedium of time, in the renewal of past memories pregnant with a host of sensations, varying from the pleasures of happy success and bright triumph, to the woe of want and failure. We will here pause only to state the recollection of one horrible scene which greeted the eyes of the young traveler while he was a reporter in Sydney. Early one morning, long before daylight, while a scribe engaged on a morning paper, he was returning from his office where he had read his last proof for the next matutinal issue, when several policemen crossed his path at a double quick pace and talking excitedly. His reportorial instinct taught him to follow them. They hastened to a disreputable quarter of the city, and entered a house around which a crowd of curious people had already assembled. They were all talking about "the villian," and indulging in the free use of strong epithets. The reporter accompanied the officers with their courteous permission, and was ushered into a large bedroom upstairs, which had been luxuriantly furnished. But the chairs were partly smashed and thrown into a heap in one corner; broken wine bottles and fragments of a large mirror were strewn over the carpet, and in the centre of the apartment lay the inanimate form of a woman with her skull literally crushed into pieces, and the brains and blood still oozing out. She was all that remained of a fallen woman. That night she had entertained the son of a well-known gambler. He had been drinking heavily, and in some unknown way she had given him offense. A quarrel ensued which led to a struggle for life, in the course of which he threw her to the floor and smashed her brains out with the heel of his boot. It was a frightful spectacle—one never to be forgotten. The wretched murderer made good his escape for a time, but was finally apprehended, though whether he was ever punished or not we do not know. Subsequent investigation by the authorities led to the discovery that the woman was of American birth. Her parents still live in Virginia, if they have not passed away very recently, and they are wealthy, worthy, and respectable. She was an only daughter, too, well educated and well brought up, but headstrong. While yet a very young woman she had married a man, whom she did not love, only to suit relatives; a little later she was the central figure of a scandal which soon got publicity through the newspapers of New York City; she deserted her home to share the fortunes of an actor, who led her astray and, in turn, deserted her. She fell lower and lower, and to hide her shame from all who had known her, fled to Australia. Her remarkable beauty was still partly preserved, and she made some money at the cost of her own loathsome misery and degradation, only to be murdered in a brothel. Such, or a similar end, is the horrible fate of thousands in Christian lands.

CHAPTER X.

Back to the Pacific Coast.—In Southern Arizona and New Mexico.—To the Sandwich Islands as a Secret Agent.—Eccentric Colonel Norris.

IT was in July, 1882, before Charles W. Hemenway reached San Francisco on his return from Australia. He brought back with him over three hundred pounds in English gold, and a week or two after his return he began to speculate in stocks on a small scale. At first he was very successful and very soon doubled his capital. Then he got a trifle less careful, and one bright morning he woke up and found himself practically penniless. Immediately he procured a loan of sufficient money, from a friend, to take him to Arizona, where he determined to retrieve his fortunes in the mines at Tombstone, then attracting some attention. The Southern Pacific Railway afforded him speedy transportation, but although he visited the Tombstone mining section, he satisfied himself by writing a description of that region and departed for El Paso, on the Rio Grande. In the meanwhile he fell back upon his pen, and once more procured a livelihood by writing. One evening, while returning from a visit to the Mexican City of Paso del Norte, located on the south side of the river, he was "held up" by a road agent, and relieved of his gold watch and rings, all of which he prized very highly because they were the gifts of friends. The country in the neighborhood of El Paso was then a sort of pandemonium. The advent of railroads had been the source of a local revolution in society and business affairs. A considerable ruffian element had drifted into the country, and robberies and even murders were of constant occurrence. Hemenway did not relish such an abnormal condition of affairs, and forthwith returned to California. By constant and hard literary labor he had been able to repay the money which he had borrowed, and to meet his every day expenses, which were very meagre at this time. But he had no surplus capital to speak of and incessant labor by day and writing by night had perceptibly injured his health. This was some time in September, 1882. An unexpected remittance, for articles sent to a Philadelphia publisher a long time before, came to his relief, and enabled him to visit Santa Cruz, a very pleasant watering place on the coast. After a short stay there, which benefitted his health very much, he once more returned to San Francisco. For a week or more he did some irregular literary work for the local press, and then he was approached by a gentleman who represented himself as an accredited agent of the Hawaiian government. This gentleman wanted a clever newspaper man to do a special service. The Planters' organization of the Islands were waging a bitter war upon the then Hawaiian adminstration, and it was feared that they contemplated revolution and bloodshed. Colonel R. Z. Spaulding was the leader of the Planters' club on the Islands. As the Planters were about to hold one of their annual conclaves, Colonel Spaulding was known to be preparing some sort of a manifesto. In order to take proper precautionary measures, the then Hawaiian administration, in the interest of peace, deemed it of importance to ascertain in advance what were the real designs of the Planters. To accomplish this purpose, the government of Hawaii wanted a discreet person to proceed as a detective, *incognito*, to the Islands. Colonel Spaulding was then advertising for a gardener, in the San Francisco papers, and it was deemed a good opportunity to get near the residence of the belligerent and dreaded Colonel. For a valuable consideration, young Hemenway undertook the service. Without exciting the suspicion of Spaulding's agent, he made a contract to proceed at once to Honolulu, and thence to Spaulding's residence on the island of Kauai, to lay out a landscape garden for the Colonel. Acting upon the adroit instructions which he received from the Hawaiian agent, everything worked like a charm. Hemenway forthwith sailed on the bark *Murray* for Honolulu. It was a peculiar voyage, and lasted eighteen days. There were a number of passengers on board who preferred to travel on a sail vessel rather than on a steamship. Among these passengers was the venerable and eccentric Colonel Norris, a notable character well known in California, where he has considerable property, and also well known in Honolulu. Mr. Norris also owns an immense tract of land in Mexico, where he once figured as a revolutionary leader, and as the consequence of a disastrous battle was driven into exile. He was then very old, and we know not whether he is alive yet or not, but he was vigorous in intellect, and knew all about everybody of any note on the Sandwich Islands. In his earlier day he had been a man of powerful physique, and even yet he had considerable strength, but he was quite deaf, and rarely conversed with anyone on that account. However, he formed a special attachment for young Hemenway, to whom he recounted the chief events of his life. He had visited the port of Honolulu forty-nine times during his life. He was an experienced navigator, and in his way a genius. He gave Hemenway a great deal of valuable information about the condition of affairs in Hawaii, and pointed out to him the path of glory for young ambition to follow there. To illustrate the Colonel's peculiar eccentricity, let us say a word about his amusements while on shipboard. He had a long line with a fish hook attached, and would silently sit and fish for hours when the bark was in a calm or moving very slowly. At other times, when the sea-gulls were following close in the wake of the vessel, he would fasten a piece of wood near the hook on his line, bait the hook with a large piece of pork, and catch gulls, draw them in, and, with shears, notch their wings like a saw; then he had some pieces of canvas cut about eight inches square, with a small slit in the middle through which he would draw the head and neck of each gull as he caught it, and then, with an air of inimitable mock solemnity that used to make the passengers roar with laughter, he would pronounce an oration dedicating the decorated gull with his clipped wings to the office of a bishop, or a "sea attorney," or a monk, or a cardinal, at the same time tossing the astonished bird out upon the water. The wings of these gulls were clipped so evenly that they could fly as well as ever, apparently; and it was not an unusual thing to see a dozen or two of them following in the wake of the bark with their cloth apron about their necks, and their notched wings showing the effects of clipping every time they attempted to fly.

After an unusually tedious voyage of some eighteen days the Islands were sighted, and the bark soon passed into the passage between the islands of Molokai and Oahu, where a provoking calm occurred. The day before a huge shark followed closely in the wake of the vessel, and Colonel Norris at once predicted that there would be a death on board. And, sure enough, while we were lying in the calm the next day, an elderly lady, returning to her home in Honolulu, expired while all alone in her state-room. When the shark first appeared, the Colonel produced a huge shark hook, which was about as large as what is known as a "hog hook" in the States. This he baited with a young pig, which had been born on board. The hook was attached to a piece of chain, which, in turn, was fastened to a large rope, and then the Colonel proceeded to fish for the shark. The huge fish came up near the surface of the water, not more than eight feet from the vessel. Over him floated two small striped fish that acted as pilot to the shark, apparently. After some little hesitation, the shark made a plunge for the pig on the hook. He seized and swallowed pig, hook and chain in an instant, and when the Colonel and several seamen undertook to pull him in, he flapped against the side of the vessel and snapped the rope that held him. But this did not dismay the shark at all. With the piece of the rope attached to the hook hanging out of his mouth, he soon reappeared very near the side of the bark. Then the Colonel got out a harpoon and drove it into the side of the shark. This time blood covered the water in the immediate vicinity of the great fish, but the rope attached to the harpoon broke, and the shark was again at liberty. After that he kept at a respectful distance from the vessel, and eventually disappeared, carrying both hook and harpoon.

CHAPTER XI.

In Honolulu.—The Kanakas.—Ah Fong, a Chinese Millionaire, and his Unfortunate Daughter.

THE next day after the *Murray* was becalmed between the islands of Molokai and Oahu, a small steamer from the Cummings' Sugar Plantation, on the east side of Oahu, hove in sight, and came alongside the bark. Her captain consented to tow the *Murray* into Honolulu harbor, and before night the bark was safely made fast alongside of the wharf, near the foot of Fourth Street. This was not the first time that young Hemenway had visited this port. In going to and returning from Australia he had stopped a few hours in Honolulu. This city is the capital of the Hawaiian kingdom, and, indeed, the only city of any importance within the realm. It is located on the south side of the Island of Oahu, upon a very capacious harbor which, however, must be entered with some care, as the channel is enfiladed with coral reefs that have more than once been fatal to the careless or ignorant mariner. The city of Honolulu stretches over a considerable extent of level and but slightly elevated country, from the beach back to the mountains, which rise to a considerable height just north of the city, and indeed form the backbone of the whole island. The population of the place will reach nearly twenty thousand altogether, over half of which is composed of natives and Chinese. The whole city is embowered in perpetual verdure. As viewed from a distance, either from the sea or from the mountains, it appears one vast arbor of foliage. Here the rose blooms in the open air all the year around, and the palm tree, the orange, fig, and banana flourish with but little care. It is a lovely spot, endowed by nature with a perfect climate of eternal summer, but unhappily blighted by a people degenerate in part and sorely afflicted. When the Islands were first discovered by Captain Cook, the natives were in a state of nature—rude and barbarian. But then they were a healthful race, perfect in physique, and free from all the taints of hereditary disease. They were called Kanakas, a name which is still applied to them, and as a people they were not wholly Indian nor akin to the negro. Their complexion was of a dark, copper color, their hair generally black and straight, but their lips were not usually as thick as those of the Ethiopian, and their intellectual development was greater. Taken all in all, Christian civilization has done an injury to the Kanakas, or at least with the progress of civilization vices and diseases have been introduced among them, and they have not only retrograded physically, but also degenerated morally. In numbers, too, they have dwindled away, and to-day there are probably not forty thousand Kanakas where there were four hundred thousand on the Islands a century or two ago. The modern Kanaka is but a feeble representative of his ancestors. Whisky and debaucheries, introduced by white men, have made sad havoc with him. Christian missionaries have despoiled him of his lands and grown wealthy upon the ruin of his fortunes. A few years ago it seemed certain that the native race of Hawaii would soon become extinct. But owing to the patriotic and noble exertions of the present chief adviser of the king, an American, named Walter Murray Gibson, the decline of the native people has been stayed. The dreadful scourge of leprosy still prevails among them, but the government is doing all in its power to eradicate the dark disorder.

The Kanaka of to-day is hospitable in the extreme. His original nature seems to have been generous to a fault. Cunning Christian missionaries, at an early day, took advantage of this noble trait to fleece and destroy him. Of late years, however, the Kanakas have learned by bitter experience to be more reserved and cautious. They have also proved themselves capable of mastering the arts of civilization, and many of the younger generation are tolerably well educated and measurably refined. They are natural musicians, and readily acquire the ability to write an elegant hand. Those who live in the city of Honolulu have adopted largely the better habits of the white men, and live very much the same as white people do, although they are still fond and even proud of many of their old ways. They also dress very much the same as their Anglo-Saxon peers do. The women are very fond of flowers, which they wear in wreaths about their necks and hats. Even the men are often decorated with these wreaths on gala occasions, and all are particularly graceful in the manner of movement and naturally fond of music, dancing and all the gay festivities known to society. Of course we are speaking of the better class of Hawaiians now. The poorer and more backward masses are not less fond of music and gaiety, but they are necessarily less accomplished and less prepossessing in appearance.

In Honolulu there is a considerable number of Europeans and Americans. These are chiefly engaged in mercantile, manufacturing and mechanical pursuits. There is not, to our knowledge, a Kanaka merchant in all the Sandwich Islands. The commerce of the kingdom is in the hands of foreigners almost altogether, and the chief taxpayers of the Islands are also foreigners. Among the wealthy foreign residents are several Chinese gentlemen who carry on an extensive business in various lines. One of these Chinese men of wealth is a central figure in the leading society of Honolulu. His name is Ah Fong. Everybody in the Hawaiian kingdom knows of this rather distinguished Celestial. Ah Fong is a typical Chinaman. He wears a cue and dresses after the fashion of his countrymen. He lives in an elegant residence, surrounded by flowers and rare tropical shrubs, trees and vines, on Nuuanu Avenue, one of the most fashionable quarters of the city. He employes white men for cooks and coachmen, keeps up a very princely establishment, and he is worth many millions of dollars. He has an interesting family, too. His wife is a half-white native woman. She has borne him many children, who are mostly grown up now. His only son was educated at Harvard University, in the United States. He is larger than his father, taller, darker and stronger. And a more able business man or a better behaved young gentleman it would be hard to find. His sisters are more delicate and by no means bad looking. They dress in the latest Parisian fashion, regardless of expense. Several of them are grown up, and they circulate in the best society. Only one of them has ever been married, and her Anglo-Saxon husband proved the superior depravity of his race forthwith. It was a sorry story. She was Ah Fong's eldest daughter, handsome and polished. A book-keeper came from the United States, and at a large salary was employed by one of the leading business houses of Honolulu. He soon obtained admittance into the most exclusive and aristocratic circles of society. His talents secured him many friends. He diligently wooed and won the daughter of the Chinese millionaire. The Celestial father was very proud of the match. The marriage ceremony was performed with much pomp and solemnity in a leading Christian church, but when the service was over the bridegroom hurried his bride into his father-in-law's carriage and drove off to his bride's residence, leaving her father to walk or get home the best way he could. The very next day the bridegroom was arrested on the very grave charge of seducing a young lady member of one of the most respectable white families in Hawaii. Forthwith he was imprisoned on the "Reef," but mysteriously escaped and fled to China. Nothing has ever been heard from him since. His wife eventually obtained a divorce from the miserable scamp, and Ah Fong and his family have given Anglo-Saxon suitors a wide berth ever since.

CHAPTER XII.

Kauai.—Kapaa.—Colonel R. Z. Spaulding.—The Condition of Laborers in Hawaii.

AFTER Hemenway had debarked at Honolulu from the *Murray*, he remained only a day or two in the city before proceeding to the island of Kauai, where the mills and plantations of Colonel R. Z. Spaulding were located. Kauai is the most northerly island of the Hawaiian group, and it is also the third in point of size, containing an area of six hundred and forty square miles. The distance from Honolulu to Nawiliwili, the nearest port on Kauai, is some eighty miles, and the journey was accomplished easily in one night on an inter-island steamer. The little port of Nawiliwili presented a picturesque appearance. Upon the left hand a narrow range of rocky mountains comes down to the water's edge. On the right hand is a barren bench, some sixty or eighty feet high, and between the mountains and the bench is a low beach sloping gradually back into a cosy little valley, where a number of native houses are located amid groves of cocoa, banana and kindred tropical trees and plants. Colonel Spaulding's plantations of Kealea and Kapaa are about ten or fifteen miles north of Nawiliwili. Hemenway found it impossible to obtain any kind of conveyance for either love or money, and leaving his baggage to be brought around the island in the course of a week or so, on the steamer, he set out on foot for Kapaa. In due time, after a tedious and dangerous journey over miserable roads, and by wading and swimming through several marshy bogs, the indomitable footman got through without much damage. Kapaa is a very small plantation village. The inhabitants were nearly all employed on the Kapaa plantation. Most of them were natives; some were Chinese; a few were *Lunas* or overseers—generally white men. At Kapaa landing were the sugar mills belonging to the plantation, together with the usual warehouses and one or two little stores. The aspect of the country thereabouts was rude and desolate in the extreme. Kealea was a place a few miles further on, and very much like Kapaa, with other sugar mills and their adjuncts. Colonel Spaulding, the proprietor of Kealea plantation and the chief owner of Kapaa plantation, had built him a handsome and commodious residence, about three miles back from the shore towards the centre of the island, in a beautiful sheltered little valley which he had reclaimed from a rude state of nature. From Kapaa to this sequestered valley residence Mr. Hemenway was conveyed in a light wagon. The Colonel and Mrs. Spaulding were absent on a visit, but Miss Ange, a French-American governess, and a number of servants received the new-comer, and domiciled him in comfortable quarters. After dinner he had time to look about and reconnoiter his position. The

Colonel's residence was erected in the centre of a little valley containing some forty or fifty acres of rich land, with a small stream of water running through it, and hills or plateaus surrounding it on three sides. It was a romantic place for a rural residence, and capable of being made a veritable paradise. Paved walks had already been laid out and roses planted. A banana grove also flourished in one corner of the valley, and down near the rivulet there was a cocoa grove. Barns and outhouses had been carefully erected, and nobody except servants lived within a mile or more of the place.

In the course of time Colonel Spaulding and his lady with three small children arrived. The Colonel was a thick-set, stolid man, with a large head, high broad forehead, cold gray eyes, a round full face, light hair, and square firm jaws. He rode about on horseback with the air of a dictator, and such he virtually was in that section of the island. His wife was a tall, rather stately woman, not over thirty years of age, and rather attractive in appearance. She had three children—two girls and a boy—the eldest not over eight years of age, and the youngest but little more than a baby. They were handsome, delicate and intelligent in a marked degree, and their nurse and governess together kept them as clean and sweet as cherubs. An accomplished Chinese cook had charge of the culinary department of the household, and a Chinese steward did the family washing and kept the large and complete domestic establishment in neatness and order. The Colonel with his family lived in princely style. Virtually he was lord over his broad acres, with no equals to question his authority or dispute his will.

Colonel R. Z. Spaulding was an American by birth. A few years before, while yet a young man, he had occupied the position of American Consul at Honolulu. At that time he was poor and unmarried. He retired from office soon. He had already made the acquaintance of his wife. She was a native of the Islands, and the daughter of an old white settler, and ex-sea captain, James McKee, who years before had located on the island of Maui, and established a romantic residence on the side of the great extinct crater, known as Haleakala. At the time of his death, Captain James McKee possessed a large property. When Colonel Spaulding married the Captain's daughter a portion of the estate came under his management. The Colonel proved himself a masterly financier. He was soon worth hundreds of thousands of dollars, and is perhaps before now a millionaire. The reciprocity treaty between the United States and Hawaii afforded him a grand opportunity to make money from the sugar industry, and he improved his opportunity splendidly.

One who has always lived in the United States, where honest labor usually confers dignity rather than social degradation and virtual serfdom, can scarcely understand the relations between servant and master in Hawaii. The chief wealth of the kingdom is derived from the cultivation of sugar-cane. The sugar plantations are mammoth establishments, owned by individual capitalists or corporations. The laborers who cultivate the soil are rarely or never land owners. They are servile hirelings in the most absolute sense of the word. Most of these laborers are South Sea Islanders, Portuguese, Chinese and Kanakas of a low class. The wages paid range from $3.00 to $10.00 per month, with a sort of board. These plantation laborers are hired on a contract system, that, under the laws of the kingdom, gives the employer the power *to force* the contracted employe to perform service for the specified length of time. If the hireling runs away, he can be arrested and brought back, fined and imprisoned, or compelled to work out the fine on the plantation. If he refuses to work, and is well, his master can apply corporeal goads to make him do his duty. This makes the contract laborer a virtual serf, and to say the truth, it would be next to impossible to cultivate sugar on the Sandwich Islands with the only labor available there, without the power which the contract system gives the employer; because the common laborers there are such an unreliable and shiftless set naturally.

The contract laborers work in gangs, on the various plantations, under the direction of bosses called *Lunas*. They are sheltered in a kind of cheap barracks, furnished them by their employers, and fed on the coarsest kind of food. The Chinese are generally considered the best hands for cane cultivation, but they demand the highest wages, and lately hundreds of Portuguese laborers have been imported. Portuguese men, women and children, as soon as the latter can handle a hoe, are all employed to labor in the cane fields, and they exhibit a patience and endurance, and humility, that is often pitiful to behold.

CHAPTER XIII.

As a Spy.—A Christmas Celebration.—As Government Inspector of Roads. —Native Habits and Costumes.

NOT long after young Hemenway had been installed on the premises of Colonel R. Z. Spaulding, he began to realize the complex and doubtful nature of his task. In the dual capacity of gardener for the Colonel and secret service agent for the government, he found his judgment taxed to the utmost. A large number of Chinamen were placed under his command to cultivate, level and lay out into a landscape garden, the spacious grounds surrounding the Spaulding mansion. And for from eight to ten hours a day he exerted himself to the utmost to make his men do the greatest possible amount of labor and to give his auxiliary employer ample satisfaction. Although he was not as skilful a gardener as he might have been, by extra application he soon won the approbation of the Colonel and his amiable lady, under whose general direction he worked. After each day's hard labor he studied and wrote at night. One or two of his contributions appeared in the Honolulu *Gazette* over his own signature. These eventually came to the notice of the Spaulding family and opened the way to his success as a secret agent. It was not long before he discovered that the Colonel had not the remotest idea of inciting a rebellion, but that his motives, while hostile to the then administration of Hawaii, were and would be kept within legitimate bounds. When this fact had been ascertained beyond the possibility of a doubt, he deemed his mission as a secret agent at an end. He did not relish the position of a spy in which he was placed. Such a position was made especially embarrassing when he was treated with such kindness and good faith by the very man whose conduct he was to observe. He therefore prepared to terminate his mission.

In the meanwhile Christmas, 1882, arrived. The day was celebrated on the Spaulding plantations in characteristic fashion. A number of horses and mules, owned by the Colonel and his various overseers or *Lunas*, were entered for a series of races on the track at Kapaa. All the inhabitants of the plantations and many natives from neighboring places gathered to witness the sport. It was the great annual event for that locality. None of the animals matched against each other on the race track were very fast, but the races were not the less exciting and amusing on that account. The Colonel furnished all the purses, and was the sole proprietor of all the affair. On Christmas evening the chief *Lunas* employed on the Spaulding plantations were invited to assemble around a Christmas tree, and partake of a Christmas banquet at the Colonel's residence. This festival was also a characteristic one. The Christmas tree was loaded down with presents for every invited guest, all purchased from the Colonel's money bags. A missionary preacher was present to say grace, the gifts were distributed in due time, and then a princely collation was served. It was a very happy household affair. For once the conventional barriers of caste between master and servant were thrown down to a certain limited extent, and unalloyed joy prevailed. Although especially invited to attend this festival, young Hemenway declined the happiness. His mission as a secret agent was about fulfilled and he was reluctant to accept the hospitality of an unsuspecting gentleman whom he had under surveillance. He remained in his room all the evening, and packed his effects preparatory to departing for Honolulu. The next morning, before he could notify the Colonel of his intended course, Mrs. Spaulding tendered him some valuable presents which had been placed upon the Christmas tree for him. This was too much for the conscience of the youthful secret agent, and he lost his self-possession, we fear. He endeavored to decline the gifts courteously, but in doing so burst into tears. Mrs. Spaulding was at once offended and astonished. A few minutes later the Colonel came in an angry mood, and declared that he would not have a man about his premises who would not accept his Christmas presents. This unexpected denouement was favorable to Mr. Hemenway's intentions. He took advantage of the opportunity to have his contract as gardener cancelled, and returned to Honolulu in a day or two.

Four months later, in the capacity of special Governmental Inspector of Roads, young Hemenway returned to Kauai, under directions from His Hawaiian Majesty's Prime Minister, Walter Murray Gibson. On this occasion, he traveled over all the roads of the island on horseback. There are six or seven sugar plantations on Kauai. The centre of the island is mountainous and inaccessible; the west coast is abrupt, high and difficult to approach from the ocean. The greater part of the soil is not adapted to the cultivation of sugar-cane. In various parts, some rice is raised by Chinamen, who monopolize the rice industry of the Hawaiian group. Sheep and cattle are also raised with success, and bananas, oranges, and a kind of apple, called *ohia*, grow spontaneously in the recesses of the mountains.

The native population of Kauai is inconsiderable. Those Kanakas who are not employed on plantations, and who own land and homes of their own, live on taro, *poi*, fish, and fruits that grow with little or no care. Taro is a vegetable which usually grows in water, some like rice. It has a root similar to that of a turnip in shape. When boiled or baked, it has a very agreeable, refreshing taste. An acre or two of taro will furnish food for a whole family, for a whole year. From taro, *poi* is manufactured by a simple process. The taro is cooked, mashed up, and allowed to foment in a calabash; then, after mixing, it is *poi*, and about as thick as the flour paste used by printers. It is of a white color, and has a tart taste. The natives eat this every day, as we eat bread. They keep it in a large calabash, around which the whole family gather at meal-time. Each individual dips his or her fingers in the dish, gathers up a quantity of the *poi*, and dexterously flings the paste-like morsel into the mouth. In the vicinity of all the islands fish are very plentiful.

The natives are expert fishermen and splendid swimmers. They go out upon the water, with nets, in small boats made of a single log, hollowed out much like an Indian canoe, and often catch large quantities of fish, with little difficulty. Generally, they prefer to eat the fish raw, although sometimes they cook it. We are speaking now of the common class of natives, in the rural districts of Hawaii, and not of the more Anglo-Saxonized native of Honolulu and vicinity.

In the country districts the natives who still own land of their own have partly discarded their old *hale pilis*, or straw thatched houses, for neat frame buildings. But still many Kanakas live in the same sort of a primitive structure as did their forefathers of centuries ago.

Nearly all the natives are good horsemen, and many of them own small herds of cattle. The Kanaka women, and for that matter some of the white ladies of Hawaiian birth, ride on horseback astride, just the same as a man does, and the spectacle of a female thus mounted is rather novel at first.

CHAPTER XIV.

Before Hon. Rollin M. Daggett.—Editor of the *Advertiser*.—His Excellency Walter Murray Gibson, a Remarkable Genius.

EARLY in January, 1883, in very indifferent circumstances, Charles W. Hemenway found himself a stranger, to all intents and purposes, in Honolulu. The agent with whom he had signed an agreement to perform secret service had up to that time failed to remit according to contract stipulations, although he subsequently made good all his promises. However, Hemenway was temporarily embarrassed financially. He had written some newspaper articles, and performed other literary labor during his leisure hours on Kauai, but some of his manuscript had been taken from him by alleged policemen just before he had departed from that island. He determined to seek redress for this outrage, through the American Minister at Honolulu. Accordingly he presented himself at the quarters of the embassy of the United States, and laid the particulars of his grievance before the Hon. Rollin M. Daggett, then Minister Plenipotentiary from this Republic, to the court of His

Majesty, King Kalakaua. Everybody in Nevada and California knows Hon. Rollin M. Daggett. Indeed, he enjoys something of a national reputation, not only as a politician and statesman, but also as an orator and polished writer.

Mr. Daggett gave Hemenway a patient hearing, and took a lively interest in his case. The facts of the seizure of the manuscript were promptly laid before the Hawaiian Prime Minister, who did his utmost to recover the property, but no trace of it could be found. The very day that Mr. Daggett laid the case before the Hawaiian government, a distinguished member of the Hawaiian Board of Health, and also manager of the *Pacific Commercial Advertiser*, the leading daily paper of Honolulu, owned by Premier W. M. Gibson, called on Mr. Hemenway at the Hawaiian Hotel and invited him to visit the office of the Minister of Foreign Affairs. The young American complied with the request, and was there first introduced to the Premier, the famous Walter Murray Gibson. With that distinguished gentleman Mr. Hemenway had a private interview of an hour's duration. When he left the presence of the Premier, the manager of the *Pacific Commercial Advertiser* immediately engaged his services as reporter.

Mr. Gibson was a remarkable man in appearance. He wore a full beard, which was iron gray; his forehead was high, capacious, and of fine texture; his large head was well covered with partially gray hair. In his younger days he had evidently been tall and graceful in person, but now his shoulders were slightly bent over, although his step was firm and elastic, and his eye keen, penetrating and fiery. The striking feature of his face was his nose, which was of the Roman type, and almost immense in its proportions. In conversation he was a perfect courtier. Every word came forth with grace and animation; every gesture was polished, and every expression bore the impression of acute sagacity and a consummate knowledge of human nature. Although so well along in years, at a glance he seemed to divine all the feelings and ambition of his much more youthful visitor, and when Mr. Hemenway left his presence he really felt as if he was under the influence of enchantment. Without having ever met Mr. Gibson, Hemenway had written some severe criticisms of his public acts as a Premier, but to these Mr. Gibson never once alluded; yet when Hemenway left His Excellency's presence, his conscience accused him of having been in the wrong in his opposition to the Premier. Such is the wonderful effect of the influence which men of genius often exercise over their fellow men.

For more than seven months Hemenway continued in Mr. Gibson's employ. In due time he became editor of the *Advertiser*, which was in reality the organ of the Hawaiian government, and the court journal of His Hawaiian Majesty, the King. Occasionally he served Mr. Gibson in the capacity of private secretary or amanuensis, and this brought him frequently to the Premier's residence, a substantial stone structure two stories high, located just west of the new theatre building, across the road from Iolani Palace, where the King dwells. Under Mr. Gibson's patronage and training, Hemenway became a pungent editorial writer, and advanced rapidly towards a success, valuable pecuniarily and in the way of experience; and for the auspicious opportunity of operating in such an instructive and remunerative sphere, Mr. Hemenway has to thank the friendly offices of Hon. Rollin M. Daggett, a gentleman of many virtues, and now an ex-envoy of excellent reputation as a diplomat; an orator and a literary master, whose genius is unquestionable and admired by all who have come within the radius of its brightness. But, though a brilliant man, Mr.

Daggett was not very handsome in person. When we first knew him he was a widower, dignified in his demeanor, social in his habits, and without many peers in conversation. He was short in statue, inclined to be a little rotund, and upon his face, which was clean-shaven, he wore an ugly scar. His hair was rather dark and besprinkled with gray. Before His Excellency was succeeded by a Democratic appointee of President Cleveland, he married a young, lovely and accomplished lady, who was born and reared in the vicinity of Seattle, Washington Territory, we believe. He brought his amiable bride to Honolulu, where she was right royally received and entertained.

The history of Walter Murray Gibson's career reads like a romance. He is an American by birth. At an early age he became an adventurer, and with a band of followers sailed out among the islands of the Pacific Ocean in quest of pleasure, profit and excitement. As the result of an ambitious effort to establish a kingdom, with himself as ruler and the natives as subjects, on the island of New Guinea, he was cast into prison where he remained about a year, and was finally rescued by a United States man-of-war. Later, some thirty years or more ago, he returned to the United States and visited Utah. While in this Territory he joined the Mormon Church, and was duly commissioned by President Brigham Young as a missionary to the South Sea Islands. He then proceeded to Hawaii, and at first met with remarkable success in introducing the Gospel, but eventually he apostatized, and several brethren were sent to depose him. He was cut off from the Church, and until some five or six years ago he lived a comparatively retired and studious life, mastering the Chinese, the Japanese and other languages. Then suddenly he emerged from his hermitage on the island of Lanai, which he owns, and offered himself as a candidate for the National Hawaiian Legislature. The idea of his success in obtaining an election was not entertained at all, but he was not discouraged. He was a perfect master of the Hawaiian language, and he went among the native voters of Honolulu district and talked to them. The strength of his eloquence—for it is admitted he used no money to promote his chances—may be conjecture from the fact that he was elected by an overwhelming majority. At once all eyes were turned upon Mr. Gibson. The organs of the Christian Missionary party, as it was called, assailed him with outrageous venom, yet he not only lived through the ordeal but actually continued to gather strength and popularity. He became proprietor of the *Pacific Commercial Advertiser*, and at once proved himself a masterly editor, overflowing with sentiments which manufactured public opinion. He was a member of the Hawaiian Legislature when the notorious Don Cæsar Celso Moreno, a brilliant but unscrupulous adventurer, succeeded in making himself Prime Minister of Hawaii, a position which he held for a month or so, and then resigned, and fled in disguise from the kingdom, to escape the wrath of the people. Soon after Mr. Gibson became Prime Minister of the realm, a position which he has filled with great ability, and which he still holds. His whole soul has been heartily devoted to the good of the Hawaiians and their perpetuity as a nation. As Premier he has labored diligently and sucessfully for the aggrandizement of the Hawaiian sovereign and kingdom. The glorious dream of his youth was the formation of a great island confederation in the Pacific Ocean, and to-day, under the patronage of King Kalakaua, he is carrying that grand plan into effect. Should his life be spared a few years more, through his exertions Hawaii will be the head of a vast Pacific Ocean Island realm that will in time be a power among the great nations of the earth, and Walter Murray Gibson will go down to history as one of the greatest statesmen of the age. In Hawaiian annals his name will be coupled with that of the native conqueror, Kamehameha, the great, who first united all the islands of the Hawaiian group under one government. Endowed with great talents and inspired with lofty ambition, Walter Murray Gibson has made many grievous blunders, but he has profitted by disastrous experience, retrieved his errors as well as possible, and ever since he has been in power in Hawaii he has befriended the native Mormons who dwell there, although they are despised and abused by the world.

CHAPTER XV.

Exceptional Opportunities.—Iolani Palace.—His Majesty King Kalakaua and Queen Kapiolani.—Punchbowl.—Laie, the Mormon Plantation..

THE position of reporter, and then the editorship of the official newspaper organ of the Hawaiian government, gave Mr. Hemenway exceptional opportunities, which he diligently improved. He had access to Iolani Palace, the large and elegant residence of King Kalakaua. He met His Majesty and Queen Kapiolani. He obtained admission, in his reportorial capacity, to court society, and formed an acquaintance with the chief officials of the realm. In early days the Hawaiian kings did not preserve much dignity, and they lived in the rude style of semi-civilized chieftains. But King Kalakaua, though a native with dark skin, is an accomplished, intelligent and scholarly sovereign, and he has placed himself in a position resembling that in which the monarchs of Europe live. He occupies the throne with dignity; his household is elaborately constituted after the fashion of royal European households, and in every external aspect he is kingly and august. Around him he has gathered the most elegant, polished and accomplished men and women of his kingdom. Foreign representatives of all the great nations of the world, and their families; distinguished foreign visitors, rich and refined residents of Honolulu, both native and naturalized, and all the wit and beauty and chivalry of the Islands, with the exception of a few hostile men who have been rancorously opposed to His Majesty's policy, were gathered around the Hawaiian throne, and constituted a court society which was really brilliant and measurably magnificent. Among such people, under the daily guidance of the experienced and courtly Prime Minister, W. M. Gibson, Charles W. Hemenway took some primary lessons in the art of a courtier, while he was daily polishing his pen and acquiring a knowledge of the world, mankind, and that sort of statesmanship of which his patron, Mr. Gibson, was the perfect embodiment. To the young American it seemed a school in which few men are privileged to study; and it afforded a kind of instruction that is very valuable to a young man who has to make his own way through life.

The best of Honolulu society is very exclusive, and on a par with the best society anywhere in the world. Nowhere on earth do ladies dress better, richer, or in more exquisite taste than among the more refined and wealthy classes of the Hawaiian capital. Nowhere on the footstool of God is life more gay, happy and gorgeous. The perennial climate of ever-blooming roses, bright skies and tropical magnificence, tempered by the vast environment of a tranquil ocean, ought to be favorable to human happiness, and so it is. But these are not the only attractions of Honolulu. Back of the city rise abruptly to a considerable height a picturesque mountain range, in the foreground of which is a novel promontory, called Punchbowl, on the top of which a few rusty old cannon slumber in the ruins of what may have been once considered a fort. Punchbowl is an extinct volcanic crater, the like of which are very numerous in Hawaii. Along the beach, a few miles east of Honolulu, is a lovely watering place or spa, called Waikiki, where the King and many wealthy merchants have lovely suburban residences. A little farther east still and Diamond Point, another rocky volcanic cone, rises from the verge of the ocean, and there are caves and grottos laved by the waves, and beautifully decorated by nature. Near Waikiki are parks of cocoa trees and palms, and also a race-course; here and there are quaint old native homes, embowered in marvelous verdure, and numerous, indeed, are the beauties of nature and scenery on every hand.

Within the city of Honolulu there are also many things which draw out the curiosity or secure the admiration of the traveler. The royal palace is a noble structure, built of stone, and some three stories high. With its surrounding grounds it occupies a whole square in the heart of the city, which is enclosed by a thick stone wall over seven feet high. Facing the palace to the south is Aliiolani Hale, a neat, large, two-story building, also environed by spacious and beautiful grounds. Aliiolani Hale is the capitol building, where all the chief offices of state are located. In front of it stands the heroic bronze statue of Kamehameha the great, the Washington of Hawaii, who flourished over a hundred years ago. All around tropical trees, artistically arranged, and various shrubbery flourish; and the place is beautiful withal.

To the north of Honolulu a road leads between a pass through the mountains, across the island. On this somewhat steep road, about six miles from the harbor, the summit of the pass is reached amid grand scenery. The descent to the north side of the island is very abrupt. On their northern flank the mountains abruptly terminate in a perpendicular wall several hundreds of feet high. A steep and narrow path, worn and cut in this rocky facade affords a passage for pedestrians and horses, but not for carriages, from Honolulu to the north side of Oahu. Standing at the top of this passage-way, the eye can scan the line of the island's northern shore for miles both east and west, and the view is unique and grand, as the ocean, six miles distant at the nearest point, fringes the varied and glorious scenery of the land with an interminable vista of ethereal blue. As the imprisoned writer sits in his cell penning these thoughts, a vivid recollection of his emotions when he first surveyed this scene, in 1883, comes back to him, and suggests the impossibility of an adequate pen picture. Again, in memory, he rides his horse down the precipitous descent which the natives call the *Pali*. Again he bounds over the undulating lower lands which are clad in a vestment of verdure, enfiladed by a gigantic perpendicular wall topped by mountain summits on the one hand, and washed by the waves on the other side. Again he reaches the northern shore of Oahu and rides from plantation to plantation, from rice field to rice field, and from native villages to the residences of richer white men. All day he spurs his horse over the island to the westward. Every mile of his progress unfolds new and striking aspects of nature to his eye. In front of him stands a great mountain promontory, which has broken out from the great stone facade of the mountains in the middle of the island and approaches the northern coast. Eventually he winds around the steep base of this grand sentinel and a new and more wide and desolate scene opens to the view.

Native settlements are fewer here, and there is no plantation for miles. At length on the northwest end of Oahu the rider reaches Laie, a considerable settlement owned and occupied by the Mormons.

When we visited this quiet place Elder Partridge was in charge. There were a number of acres of sugar-cane almost ready to cut and a mill on the plantation was provided with the machinery for manufacturing sugar. Laie embraces a large section of land that might be profitably utilized for cane-growing if it was not for a scarcity of water for irrigating purposes. A large number of natives of the Mormon faith lived on the plantation, which also embraces some fine rice lands that were leased by Chinamen. A large artesian well had then lately been sunk on the premises, which went a great way toward irrigating some of the rice and taro lands. We met Elder Partridge in the new meeting house which he was just completing on the premises, and for part of a day we were his guests. He lived upon a low bench, in an old frame house comfortably furnished and located half a mile or so from the ocean shore. Soon after our visit the new church was dedicated with much solemnity, and His Majesty, the King, was present on the occasion, by the advice of his Prime Minister, Mr. Gibson. By the expenditure of a few thousand dollars, Laie might be made one of the most pleasant spots on the island. As it is there is an air of barrenness about it, but the natives who live there were well taken care of and happy. A few miles east of the plantation there are several other Mormon native settlements, and there must be more than a thousand Mormon natives in that locality. They live a quiet, easy life, help to cultivate the plantation lands, from the products of which many of them are fed, and also engage in fishing frequently.

The route around Oahu, from Laie along the western end of the island, south to the southern shore, and thence back to Honolulu, is more or less rough. Immediately west of Laie is a tract of sand hills, and then the low ground between the mountains and the shore for miles is inhabited only by a few natives, with here and there the residence of a white settler, engaged in the cattle business, which is quite profitable here. On the southwest side of the island there are two large sugar plantations near the shore, and between them and the mountains, extending towards Honolulu, is a plateau which is only available for grazing purposes. No person should visit the

Hawaiian islands without making the round of Oahu, at least, on horseback. A good horse will accomplish the journey easily in two days, and the people, both native and foreign, are hospitable and accommodating.

CHAPTER XVI.

Coronation of King Kalakaua.—Among would-be Revolutionists.—Speech-making for his Life.—A Suicide.

DURING the earlier months of Mr. Hemenway's residence in Honolulu, the coronation of King Kalakaua took place. His Majesty had been elevated to the kingly office some years before, but the customary ceremonial of a coronation had not taken place. Eventually however, the Legislature appropriated some $10,000 for the expenses of a proper coronation ceremony, which took place in February, 1883. As court reporter, Mr. Hemenway wrote an elaborate account of this rather happy and grand event, which originally appeared in the *Pacific Commercial Advertiser* and which was afterwards printed in neat pamphlet form together with some introductory matter dictated to the reporter by His Excellency, Mr. Gibson. At the time the coronation took place some of the journals of the United States were inclined to ridicule the affair, but from all we can glean from accounts of similar events in the old world, the coronation ceremonies and festivities of his Hawaiian Majesty were in full accord with the usages and the pomp of such occasions, and fully in keeping with the spirit and style of the coronations of the most powerful European potentates. Of course it was not such an expensive or elaborate and magnificent display as that which might be made in honor of the coronation of a Russian Czar, or a King of England, but it was a brilliant consummation for Hawaii. War vessels and embassies of Great Britain, the United States, France, Japan and numbers of the greatest nations of the earth came to pay homage to the Hawaiian King, and were at Honolulu when the great event took place. The dawn of the coronation day was ushered in with salvos of artillery; later in the day an immense procession formed and marched to the grounds of Iolani Palace, where a gigantic amphitheatre had been erected to accommodate spectators; the ceremony of crowning the sovereign then took place, in the presence of the assembled multitude, the royal family and the notables of the kingdom. The crown was placed upon His Majesty's brow by Chief Justice Judd, and the peculiar royal robe of feathers, an old Hawaiian emblem of royalty, was buckled upon his shoulders. The Queen, Kapiolani, was similarly invested with the insignia of sovereignty. The Royal Hawaiian Band, than which there is no better in the world, perhaps, discoursed its choicest strains at appropriate intervals, and nothing was wanting to make the event a success in its way. In the evening, the palace grounds were thrown open; the crest of Punchbowl and the neighboring mountains were illuminated with fireworks, which were also exploded on the premises of the palace until away after midnight. At the same time invited guests from abroad, the representatives of foreign governments in Honolulu, and the rank, wealth, beauty and chivalry of the whole kingdom joined in a ball in the magnificent halls of the palace, while on the grounds native *hula hula* dancers, in their peculiar costumes, performed for the amusement of the multitude assembled around the royal residence, where night was turned into a wierd dream by oriental illuminations. It was an occasion which can never be forgotten by those who witnessed it as the writer did.

The event of the coronation did not please all of the residents of Honolulu. In that city there are always a large number of nondescript white men, of indifferent characters, who drive coaches, perform skilled labor and "rustle" for a livelihood. A few of the more intelligent and ambitious of this class conceived the idea of overthrowing the native King and putting a white man in Kalakaua's place. An old American gentleman, who had lived on the Islands upwards of thirty years, and who had conceived an unconquerable hate for the Kanakas generally, was at the head of this movement. He kept a sort of a public house which was the rendezvous of common laborers, and there the conspiracy was partly hatched. The movement seemed to fascinate those to whom it was proposed, and in less than a month the cause had over five hundred adherents, nearly all of whom were ready to shoulder a musket and march on the palace. As Kalakaua had only a handful of soldiers, of course he could not have defended himself, nor could a white man have been placed upon the throne, for the reason that some foreign nation would have been sure to have interfered in behalf of the hereditary ruler. But this did not deter the revolutionists. Under the guise of forming a labor society, they finally held a great mass meeting at the Hawaiian Hotel. Just before this occurred, Hemenway was let into the secret of the affair, and promptly conveyed the intelligence to Mr. Gibson, for the plan was to assassinate the Premier. Mr. Gibson instructed him to attend the meeting and participate. He did so, and was elected secretary. In the course of the evening he made a speech. A temporary organization was effected, with Hemenway still in the position of secretary. The next night the leaders of the conspiracy invited him to meet them in secret conclave. In the meanwhile he was duly commissioned a secret agent of the government, by Mr. Gibson, and under his instructions took down a brief sketch of the plans which the leading revolutionists unfolded to him. He tried to dissuade them from such a bloody undertaking, but they had become infatuated, and only accused him of being afraid. With the names of the conspirators all in hand, and a full knowledge of all their schemes, he withdrew from them and in conjunction with Mr. Gibson took measures to dissolve the traitorous organization. This was accomplished very quickly and very quietly. A number of the ringleaders of the proposed revolt were informed privately that a full knowledge of their schemes was in the hands of the government, and unless they left the city they would be punished. This was all that was necessary. The whole business was instantly broken up. Some of the leading conspirators were not satisfied, however, and they invited Hemenway to meet them at Brewer's Hall. He received the summons late one night, while reading the last proofs for the morning's issue of the *Advertiser*, and immediately he repaired to the hall. On the way there, a big negro pounced upon him with a knife, and threatened to launch him into eternity, but the would-be assassin was held back by companions. At the hall, Mr. Hemenway faced the exasperated revolutionists, and in reply to their accusations of treachery, and to allay a burning spirit of fury, he was compelled to make another speech, in which he boldly acknowledged his action, and then defended it with such success that the majority were convinced that he had acted with a true regard not only for humanity but also for their own particular interests, safety and welfare. The effort which that address cost the young man was such that he could not have made it, had he not felt that his life depended upon the impression he could make with language, his only weapon of defense. Under a strain of excitement that can be better imagined than described, he left Brewer's Hall that night, and proceeded at once to Mr. Gibson's residence, and reported the matter to him. His Excellency seemed rather pleased with the news; he declared that the revolutionary movement was finally baffled, and congratulated his servant.

The next day Mr. Hemenway was despatched on a special mission to the islands of Maui and Hawaii. He left in the afternoon on a little inter-island steamer. Among the passengers on board was the wife of Doctor Agnew, a gentleman who had settled in Honolulu a few years before, and accumulated a handsome fortune. That very day, in the morning, Mrs. Agnew had arrived from Australia, where her husband had left her some years before, but the Doctor not only neglected to receive her affectionately, but he declined to recognize her. It was understood that she had been unfaithful to him once, and also acquired a habit of drinking. The woman remained in Honolulu during the day, because there was no way to leave, and, with perfect composure, boarded the little island steamer in the evening. When the vessel had got out beyond Diamond Point, just after sundown, Mrs. Agnew went below into the cabin, and brought a bottle of wine on deck, from her valise. She drank all of the contents, sat down on the taffrail a moment, arranged the folds of her rich, white, silk dress, and then suddenly, and without a word of warning, sprang overboard. The sea was rough, and although the steamer was stopped at once and boats lowered, she was never seen again. It is probable that she was drawn into the screw propeller, and killed in an instant; and then the sharks, which are numerous in the vicinity of the Islands, probably devoured her remains.

CHAPTER XVII.

Maui and Hawaii.—Claus Spreckels and Spreckelsville.—Haleakala.—Kilauea.—The Legend of the Beautiful Hawaiian Princess.

THE islands of Maui and Hawaii lie in a southeasterly direction from Honolulu. The island of Hawaii is, by great odds, the largest in all the Sandwich group; it gives its name to the whole archipelago; for among the residents of the Kanaka kingdom the appellation "Sandwich" is never used, but instead thereof

"Hawaiian" is substituted as the general name of the entire realm. Maui is the second largest of these islands. By sea it is something like one hundred miles from Honolulu to Lahaina, the first landing place and settlement on Maui, where the steamer from the capital city touches to land passengers and freight. The sun was just rising in unclouded splendor back of the mountains east of Lahaina when our little steamer hove to and lowered boats to land passengers at this place. The scene was a beautiful one. On one side were the mountains of Molokai and Maui, and on the other side, at some distance, was the low coast of Lanai, a small island owned by His Excellency W. M. Gibson, and chiefly devoted to grazing of sheep and cattle. Over the whole vista of ocean, land and mountain, the sun threw his golden beams with almost magic effect.

Mr. Hemenway did nót land at Lahaina, but he proceeded further on to about the centre of the southern coast of Maui and there debarked, took a conveyance and rode across the island to Wailuku and Spreckelsville. Very lofty mountains occupy both the northwest and southeast ends of Maui, but the middle of the island is a low table-land, and the ride from the south side of the island to Wailuku bay and plantation on the north side of the island may be readily accomplished over excellent roads in an hour or so. From Wailuku harbor Claus Spreckels and his brothers have constructed a narrow gauge railway to their vast sugar mills at Spreckelsville, some ten or twelve miles distant. The great German-American capitalist, Claus Spreckels, has done more for the Hawaiian islands in the way of developing her sugar resources and commercial capabilities than any other living man. Owing to his gigantic enterprise, thousands of acres of valuable land that had laid for centuries almost a barren waste, have been transformed into the best cane-producing soil that the world affords. He has brought water from the mountains and irrigated this extensive region, which thus sprang from worthlessness into valuable fertility at once; but not without a vast expenditure of labor and treasure. In the midst of this redeemed waste stands Spreckelsville, a monument to the enterprising genius of Claus Spreckels. The town consists entirely of the residences of the laborers employed by Claus Spreckels and company, together with the five or six mammoth sugar mills, all supplied with the most perfect machinery known to modern times. Claus Spreckels and his brothers are interested largely in other

Hawaiian plantations; they have established the Oceanic Steamship Company, which built and is now running a line of magnificent American-built steamships between Australia, Honolulu and San Francisco. In the Hawaiian capital Claus Spreckels has erected a palatial residence second only to the royal palace in size and grandeur; but Spreckelsville is by far the greatest monument of his industry, enterprise and great financial ability. One who has never seen sugar manufactured on a large scale can profitably spend a whole week in Spreckelsville. As the millionaire proprietor has vast financial interests in San Francisco, he is not to be found on his plantation at all times by any means; in fact he but rarely visits Spreckelsville nowadays, but Mr. Hemenway chanced to meet him there.

Claus Speckels, the capitalist king of Hawaii, is a German by birth, and an American citizen by naturalization. He is probably in the neighborhood of fifty years of age, although he does not look that old. About medium height and rather stoutly built, with light hair, and a cast of countenance peculiar to the better class of Germans, his eyes glisten with intelligent penetration and his manner is brisk and lively. In conversation he is all that one would expect a far-seeing and great financier to be. Personally, in society he is convivial, congenial and generous. He has an amiable wife, also of German parentage, and a number of most interesting children of superior appearance. His history unfolds one of the financial marvels of the nineteenth century. Years ago he came to the Pacific coast, a poor but an honest and industrious youth. By the sheer force of his great ability, rather than by any stroke of happy fortune, he has worked his way up to a leading position among the greatest princes of industry and commerce in all the world. Hawaii may consider herself fortunate in that much of her material resources are in the keeping of Claus Spreckels.

Immediately southeast of Spreckelsville, Haleakala, the largest extinct crater in the world, rears its gigantic proportions more than ten thousand feet into the sky. About the base of this stupendous mountain there is excellent pasturage during most seasons of the year; upon the top of the massive barrier, in the old crater, there is now a forest in place of the lava fires which used to rage there ages ago. On the southwest side of Haleakala is the famous and beautiful old McKee homestead, with its lovely parterres, magnificent groves, cosy home and unique surroundings. Here Captain James McKee, a veteran sea commander, settled years ago and founded one of the most inviting rural abodes in all Hawaii. He is dead now, and his scarred remains sleep in a mausoleum erected amid the groves and gardens that he planted on the homestead which will long be his best monument.

After paying a flying visit to the inviting place, Mr. Hemenway re-embarked on an inter-island steamer and proceeded southwest, passing along the entire western coast of the great island of Hawaii, which is some four thousand square miles in area. This western coast is a vast wall of lava, rising some hundreds of feet and sloping back with more or less precipitation to an impenetrable forest which crowns the centre of the island. At some remote period, Hawaii was a great mass of flowing lava, as its whole formation still testifies. Gradually, time has worn away the rocks, and vegetation has appeared in the valleys and on the more level tracts where many large plantations now thrive, but still the western coast is comparatively barren, and rarely anything but native settlements and small cultivated plats are to be seen there. In the little ravines worn in the rock by the action of the elements for centuries, the Kanakas cultivate taro and bananas and delicious pineapples. In places the cocoanut tree rears aloft its characteristic top upon its branchless stalk, and in this vicinity the celebrated Kona coffee is raised. Along this coast, also, is the gloomy, rocky little bay upon the margin of which the renowned English navigator and explorer, Captain Cooke, was killed some three centuries past. Near the spot where he fell, the British government has erected a monument to his memory, which we gazed upon with curiosity, and which recalled to our mind many historical pictures of the distant and romantic "long ago," when the great Pacific Ocean was a region of partial myth and many wonders.

Down in the southwestern part of the coast line of Hawaii, there is a break in the lava bed wall enfilading the shore. Here is the landing of Hancaupo, in the vicinity of two small plantations. A few miles back in the interior the great back of Mauna Loa can be seen rising more than thirteen thousand feet above the sea level. And a little south and east of Hancaupo, flaring up into the sky, from an extension of Mauna Loa, may be seen the light of the volcano of Kilauea, which, at the time of our visit, was very active. Here Hemenway disembarked once more. An excellent saddle horse was in waiting for him; he proceeded to visit the neighboring thrifty sugar plantations, and spent a day among the mountains. The scenery was magnificent from many points back in the interior a few miles. In the evening, in company with some American gentlemen employed as book-keepers and time-keepers on the plantations, Hemenway visited the Haneaupo beach in the moonlight. There he witnessed a novel scene which may be called a native fishing excursion. In the ocean, a few rods from shore, were forty or fifty native men, women and children, of all ages, swimming about like a school of porpoises, and drawing in a net which had already been "set" for snaring fish. Nothing could exceed the graceful dexterity of the lithe and supple swimmers, as they moved about through the waves, endeavoring, by splashing and diving, to drive the fish into their net. The dark, copper colored bodies of some of the natives glistened in the moonlight; in the surrounding ocean the stars of heaven were mirrored; for the weather was calm and the sea almost as smooth as glass; the rugged adjacent features of the island were outlined in the poetical and bright stillness of the night; the surf broke in barely audible ripples on the rocky beach, and all nature seemed like a poem, while away off in the distance the volanic fires of Kilauea threw a great lurid light athwart the heavens, which modified the hue of the moon's pale beams, and gave the scene a still more wonderful grandeur.

The next day the young traveler proceeded to the volcano on horseback. It was a long, dreary ride. Kilauea is approached from this side over a great hard and broken mountain side of lava formation. The great black crater, with its red hot boiling lakes of molten rock, is a sight that no description can portray in all its awful grandeur, although many eloquent and masterly pens have undertaken to paint the scene in well-chosen words. We will not attempt the task of describing the volcano, because of the certainty that we could but do its wonders greater injustice.

Kilauea has been an active volcano continuously, ever since history has had any record of its existence. However, native Kanaka traditions say that there was a time when Kilauea was a great barren rock, without the sign of any volcanic phenomenon. But, in an ancient and fabulous age, a beautiful Hawaiian princess was born. Her royal parents reared her tenderly in the lap of luxury, and she blossomed forth into the perfection of womanly glory. Her complexion was but a shade darker than the olive; her eyes were large and as lustrous as the stars of heaven; her form was stately, soft, and voluptuous; her hands and feet small and delicate, and her fingers long and symmetrical. Withal, she was a supremely delightful embodiment of intoxicating female loveliness, and her hair was—red. Naturally the noble youth of the land vied with each other desperately to win the hand of the lovely princess. Although many of her native suitors sacrificed their lives as a testimony of their devotion, still she was not moved to love. But presently a beautiful white youth appeared mysteriously on the Islands. He came from the Land of the Morning; his brow was white as snow, and his lips like red roses. Instantly the princess lost her heart; for months she wooed the white boy, but, alas! in vain—she could not captivate him, and her disappointed love at last drove her into desperation. Finally she summoned all the beauty and gallantry of Hawaii to assemble for a great festival in a rustic retreat under the brow of Kilauea. The occasion was celebrated with games and dancing, and the lovely princess appeared in all the grandeur of her rank and beauty, to make one last attempt upon the wonderfully fair but indifferently inclined white youth of the Morning. In the middle of the day, when the festival was at its height, the princess had occasion to retire to a secluded bower to arrange her toilet, and there, to her great astonishment and chagrin, she discovered the fair young stranger of her fancy in the fond embrace of an ugly maiden of ignoble birth. At the sight of this spectacle the affection in the heart of the princess turned to bitter hate, and a jealous fury seized her soul. She fled to the spot where the volcano of Kilauea now is, and there nourished her passions of jealousy and hatred into such a flame that her lovely person took fire and communicated the consuming blaze to the rocks upon which she sat. Thus was the heart of the mountain first ignited with the everlasting fire which melts the elements in the bosom of Kilauea until this day.

CHAPTER XVIII.

Back again to Native Land.—Editor of the Salem, Oregon, *Talk*.—A Rustic journey to Baker City.—In Boise City, Idaho.

RETURNING from the volcano of Kilauea, Hemenway re-embarked at Haneaupo and continued his excursion, touching at Hilo and several other small ports, and eventually returning to Honolulu, where he again resumed the editor's chair in the office of the *Daily Advertizer*. After the lapse of a month or so, he again visited various islands in a semi-official capacity, and late in the fall of 1883 he severed his connection with Premier Gibson, and departed for the Pacific coast and his native land once more. Early in the winter he left San Francisco for Portland, Oregon, and for four months he taught school in the country some miles from the Oregon metropolis. In the spring of 1884, he appeared in Salem, the beautiful capital city of Oregon. Here he was promptly engaged as editor-in-chief of the *Daily Talk*. By unflagging exertion, he succeeded in giving this paper a fresh lease of life. His residence in the web-foot capital was altogether a happy one. Taken all in all, the residents of Salem are a select people. Socially they are pure, refined, intelligent and accomplished, as a rule, which holds entirely good in respect to the better classes of the place, who are vastly in the majority. Mr. Hemenway remembers with the liveliest sentiments of esteem Governor Moody, Secretary of State Earhart, and his assistant F. E. Hodgskin, County Recorder Chamberlane, Hon. Tilford Ford; capitalist and banker, A. Bush, Hon. Leo Willis and many other foremost citizens, to whom he is indebted for kindly appreciation and good will and even more substantial recognition. He remembers also with a feeling of respect and admiration the members of the Alka-Hesperian Society, a large and flourishing organization embracing the young gentlemen and ladies of the best families in the city. This society is devoted to literary and social pursuits. A more pure, bright, congenial and refined association of young people never came under our observation.

In Salem all the great State institutions of Oregon are located. There, also, are the celebrated Willamette University and Sacred Heart Academy, both educational establishments of the first excellence. Salem is built upon a level plat of land, on the east side of Willamette River, in a prolific valley of the same name. Its streets are broad and regular, and it probably now claims a population of nearly ten thousand souls. In summer time, and during the early part of fall and the latter part of spring, the climate is delightful, and while the numerous shade trees that enfilade the streets retain their leaves and the many lawns and gardens their foliage, Salem is one of the most charming cities of the country. A great many of her citizens are retired merchants and professional men, and these give a kind of conservative tone to society there.

During the latter part of July, 1884, Mr. Hemenway retired from the editorship of the *Daily Talk*. His health had been materially effected by incessant application to the duties of his editorial position. He had tried with eminent success to lift up the fortunes of an unfortunate paper. Others had monopolized the chief pecuniary benefit, and he deemed it due to himself to take a vacation. At first he went to The Dalles; there after a short stay he fitted himself out with a saddle horse and pack animal and started across the country, two hundred miles, to the headwaters of the John Day and Malheur rivers, with rifle and fishing tackle, for a genuine summer outing. The surface of the country from The

Dalles through to John Day Valley, and thence to Baker City, in western Oregon, is extremely rough, seamed with immense gorges and broken plateaus, with here and there a level section or a small fertile valley. We remember particularly the awful gorge through which the Deschutes River passes, where the Canyon City road crosses it. For a number of miles the traveler passes over a rolling, gradually ascending, and finally almost level country, and then he suddenly arrives at a great, deep opening in the earth's surface, down which the road leads precipitously for over five miles before the bottom is reached. Standing at the top of this gigantic declivity, the scene is peculiarly grand and impressive. In the distance the great white head of Mt. Hood is visible, and for miles to the westward the surface of the soil seems to be in chaos. It is a diverting, healthful exercise to travel through this wild region. Hemenway finally reached the wooded mountains near and between the sources of the John Day and Malheur rivers, and there in the solitary seclusion of the wilderness he pitched his tent, and for two months subsisted on fish, venison, bacon and "flapjacks" cooked by his own hands. During that time he never saw but one human being, and that was a hunter who was too far distant to hail. For Hemenway there was a fascinating kind of wild freedom and transport in such a life. Daily he made long excursions through the forest in search of game and to commune with nature. There is a sort of inspiration in the deep mountain jungles, where the foot of man has never or seldom trod. There is a kind of solemn society in the silence of nature where none intrude but the guests of fancy and thought and retrospection. With his brief but checkered and eventful past to ponder over, Charles W. Hemenway enjoyed this situation as perhaps few men could. The altitude of the place where he had camped was high, and by the first of October the weather began to get very cold. This made it necessary to repair to the confines of civilization. Baker City, eighty-five or ninety miles distant, was the nearest town of any note. Thither the traveler repaired, and disposing of his horses, he went by stage to Boise City, the capital of Idaho, where he at once procured a position on the editorial staff of the *Idaho Statesman*.

At that time the notorious William Bunn was Governor of Idaho Territory; the Legislature was about to assemble in Boise, and political intrigue was the order of the day. Theodore F. Singiser, a Republican, had just been beaten by honest

John Hailey, a Democrat, for Territorial Delegate to Congress; the Mormon problem had been thrust into the issue of the recent local campaign, and as a consequence old political parties were more or less demoralized. Mr. Hemenway's position on the *Statesman* threw him into the midst of the political whirlpool. No one who has always spent his life in Utah, or who has never taken any part in the typical political agitations of the day in the United States, can possibly comprehend the character of the coterie of politicians which gathered around the Idaho capital to anticipate the forthcoming meeting of the Legislature, and as far as possible forecast its action. Everybody had an ax to grind, and nobody seemed very particular about any principle or the public welfare, if he could only make money. Finally the Legislature did assemble. The great majority of the members of both branches of this "Idaho Parliament" were very commonplace and grossly ignorant. To this rule there were a few brilliant exceptions. Representative McKern, of Nez Perce County, was an able speaker and a scholarly lawyer and gentleman. The council could boast of three bright members, namely, Silas W. Moody, James E. Hart and Speaker Wood. But altogether the whole Legislature was rather a tame uninspired body, and it speedily became the mere tool of a sharp little ring of Federal wire-pulling schemers. This ring was headed by the then Territorial Secretary, D. P. B. Pride, ably seconded by Governor Wm. M. Bunn and lesser official luminaries. Pride represented the brains of the coterie. The anti-Mormon test oath law passed by the Legislature was really a conception of his. He was a Republican and had an eye to the future Congressional Delegateship of Idaho. The Territory was, however, hopelessly Democratic, and he promptly conceived the brilliant idea of reversing its political complexion by defranchising the Mormon voters of Idaho, who always had cast their ballots with the Democracy. But although this idea was original with Pride, many of his fellow carpet-bag statesmen speedily adopted it, and the then United States Marshal, Fred. T. Dubois, has anticipated Pride's ambition to take advantage of the famous test oath law, for the purpose of attempting to secure an election on the Republican ticket as Delegate to Congress. Pride "ran" the Legislature, however, and for his benefit that body created the office of Territorial Prosecuting Attorney, and put him into it. In beautiful legislative schemes of this sort, the *Idaho Statesman* of Boise City took a hand, and its proprietor insisted upon going into so many questionable issues that Mr. Hemenway, as his literary instrument, felt constrained to retire from the *Statesman's* editorial staff, which he did forthwith by a peremptory resignation January 1, 1884. A day or two later he departed from Idaho for Utah.

CHAPTER XIX.

In Utah at Last.—Payson a Place of Destiny.—In Love.— The Result.

ALL over the world Utah and the Mormons enjoy a co-ordinate celebrity. The Territory of Utah is a Territory of marvels; and the Mormons, who have founded their homes and temples here are a marvelous people. The practice of plural marriage, commonly called polygamy, has given them a world-wide notoriety; and fabulous accounts of their character and religion have filled the public mind with curiosity respecting them. So erroneous and distorted are the average popular opinions concerning these people, that we have heard a New England school mistress enquire, in all soberness, whether or not the polygamists had horns or looked at all like other people. Naturally enough Mr. Hemenway was anxious to get somewhat acquainted with this remarkable people called Mormons. While in Idaho he had read some of their ecclesiastical works, and also made the acquaintance of Hon. James E Hart, then a Mormon member of the Idaho Legislature from Bear Lake County, in the southeastern corner of the Territory. Mr. Hart was the son of polygamous parents, and yet he was a most exemplary, intelligent and companionable young gentleman. Owing to his representations of the habits and characteristics of his people, Mr. Hemenway determined to settle in Utah. He had tired of change, and accumulated a considerable experience, which had taught him something of the hollowness of fame, glory and ostensible eminence in various walks of life. He had discovered that the most glowing honors were usually attained at great sacrifice, and frequently worn with pain and sorrow. He had learned that even the prominence which the noblest ambition might attain brought with it a train of cares, perplexities and dangers. He had seen, also, much of corruption and depravity in high places, among the rich, the grand, the learned and the wealthy everywhere he had been. He no longer sought the glare of publicity, nor did he covet renown or the applause of a thoughtless and selfish world any more. The chimerical aspirations of his early days had been modified by the knowledge that a few stern eventful years nad brought, and his heart yearned for the quiet and peaceful joys of a retired and simple rustic home, where he might surround himself with pure and honest friends, with no invidious distinctions or shallow conventionalities or spiteful ambitious jealousies to introduce one element of hell. Having in vain sought for a paradise of earthly happiness among the glare, pride, fashion, wealth and power of men and communities, he now turned back to seek the object of his pursuit in sequestered obscurity, and a retired existence among the meek and lowly.

Animated by such a sentiment, early in January, 1884, Charles W. Hemenway passed through Ogden to Salt Lake City, where he remained a few days to select an inviting rural locality to settle in. He then found his current funds in danger of being exhausted, and wrote to a relative with whom he had deposited a neat little sum a year or two before. A week passed by but the relative failed to respond. The Federal authorities of the Territory had just begun a vigorous prosecution of Mormons who lived in the habit and repute of plural matrimony, and it was impossible for a stranger to obtain, from Mormon sources, any valuable information as to the most inviting localities for residence among the country settlements; so, as a matter of economy, to select a rural place of abode, and to write a few articles for a Chicago paper, Mr. Hemenway left Salt Lake City on the D. & R. G. Railway. He stopped a few days at Lehi, at American Fork, at Provo and at Springville, daily expecting a remittance from the custodian of the money which he had laid by for a rainy day, but none came, and he had but a few dollars left while he found himself in a land of strangers who regarded him with the utmost suspicion - as they then did all new-comers—because of the general dread of "spotters," "spies," and the like, who were supposed to be in search of evidence against polygamists. Under these circumstances, he set out on foot in quest of work of any kind to enable him to sustain himself until he could procure his funds. Everywhere he found many idle men and no employment to be obtained at any rate. The affair was getting desperate. His purse was about all empty. He had traveled about through the mud to get work for several days indefatigably, and was almost worn out when he reached Payson, a settlement of about two thousand five hundred inhabitants, somewhere about seventy miles south of Salt Lake City. When he first came in sight of Payson, it was raining and snowing alternately. He sat down on a fence rail to deliberate and rest a few moments, for he was very tired. For half an hour or so he was lost in thought, and then he suddenly looked up and noticed that the clouds had cleared away and left Payson in the sunshine. A peculiar feeling came over him, and he said to himself: "I will go no further than that settlement; there I will meet my destiny; I believe there is something there for me." Forthwith he dismounted from the fence and struggled through the mud a mile or two until he reached the village, where he found a home-like country hotel kept by Mr. Robert Smith, and secured supper and lodging for the night. The next day he undertook the almost impossible task of obtaining some sort of employment. No one thereabouts at that season of the year had any work to do, or if they had they would not have hired a stranger to have done it. But true to his determination Hemenway refused to entertain a thought about going on further, and after a few days Orrawell Simons, Sr., an old and well-to-do resident of the place, took the young stranger into his own house, and offered him board and lodging for what little miscellaneous labor he could perform. For over a month Hemenway remained with Mr. Simons, cutting wood with an ax, feeding stock and the like. During this time he had plenty of leisure to observe the peculiarities and characteristics of the Mormon people by whom he was entirely surrounded. He was profoundly impressed by the simple candor and indubitable sincerity of all the masses of the Latter-day Saints. He was thoroughly convinced that they were conscientious in their belief in plural marriage. He mingled with them freely and familiarly in many instances, and attended their religious meetings on many occasions to satisfy himself respecting them. Among the Latter-day Saints of Payson, at that time, the penetrating observer could not fail to recognize a sentiment of social harmony and union that is generally alien to society throughout the Christian world. And, without having decided to join the Mormon Church, Hemenway determined to remain among these peculiar people. He was tired of the excitements of city life; the toils of a newspaper avocation no longer had any fascination for him, and he began to lay plans for establishing himself in the possession of a rustic home, a few acres of land, and some cattle and sheep to keep him busy. In the meanwhile chopping wood seemed to agree with him; he grew strong and hearty; his hands began to get hard and his features tanned and weather-beaten. He began to flatter himself that he would soon make a typical ranchman, farmer, or stock-raiser. But, alas! how little men know which way they are drifting. The poet has well said:

> "There is a destiny that shapes our ends,
> Rough-hew them as we may."

One evening at a joint meeting of the Mutual Improvement Associations of Payson, Hemenway noticed a young lady who seemed to him extremely lovely. He had never seen her before, but for hours and days afterwards the soft and amiable outlines of her face would intrude upon his fancy. A few weeks later he saw her face once more, but he did not speak to her and she scarcely noticed him. With his rude overalls and long hair he was not an ideal lover, perhaps, but nevertheless from the moment he saw the young lady the second time he was in love, entirely and absolutely, for the first time in his whole life. A great, deep, all-pervading passion seized his heart just as great affections do, once in a lifetime. He enquired who the young lady might be that had been the thoughtless inspirer of such profound emotions. Miss Ireta Dixon was the poetical name which the villagers said was hers. Hemenway did not ask for an introduction; he merely determined that Miss Dixon should be his wife, and said nothing. Then he found that he already had many rivals although at that time no one ever dreamed the secret of his inmost soul. "Ah," thought he, "I must act promptly or I shall be too late;" and that afternoon of the third Sunday in February he abolished all the plans which he had been maturing for a month, and, with all his characteristic energy, besought himself how he might most quickly win the hand and heart of the fair-haired, brown-eyed Ireta. That very night, amid snow and mud, and with a small bundle of clothes packed upon his back, he set out on foot for Provo, twenty miles distant. "If I win that bonny girl," thought he, "I must speedily put myself in a condition to command respect and a suitable income." Again the old fondness for the editorial sanctum came back to him as he tramped through the mud and sleet during the whole of that dark and stormy night, but with the old professional fondness there was a new light, a new inspiration, a new and hallowed love which went out from the midnight pedestrian's heart towards the remembered features of a blithe country girl, to whom he was a total stranger and yet to whom he owed one of the most powerful and ennobling of all the impulses that can thrill and exalt the soul of a strong, earnest man.

CHAPTER XX.

Prove City.—Installed in the *Enquirer* Office.—Editor of the Ogden *Daily Herald.*—Married.—To Ireta.

PROVO is a very lovely little city of some five or six thousand inhabitants, hardly forty miles south of Salt Lake City, in Utah Valley. It is a quiet, orderly and pleasant place to live in, but during the month of February, 1884, it was anything but an inviting centre of business activity. After his night's forced march through the mud from Payson, Hemenway found himself in the suburbs of Provo about daylight Monday morning. During the night his clothes had been soaked with melting sleet repeatedly, but towards morning the weather had turned cold, and soon his outer garments were frozen upon his back. Cold, hungry and tired, indeed, was he, that bleak and disagreeable morning, but he was not one whit discouraged. The streets of the city were all deserted when he first arrived, and he paced up and down the railway platform until about nine o'clock, when he called on Mr. Harvey H. Cluff, one of the Presidency of Utah Stake. This gentleman Mr. Hemenway had casually met before. Mr. Cluff was found at his office near the Utah Central Railway depot. He was very kind to the young man, and evidently comprehended a part of his circumstances, for, without being asked, he loaned Mr. Hemenway $2.50 to be repaid when convenient. Then Hemenway proceeded to a hotel and got a late but highly acceptable breakfast. It gives a man an appetite to walk all night in the mud and cold. The balance of the day was spent in searching diligently for employment, though none was found. But before another twenty-four hours elapsed, through the friendly offices of the President of the Stake, Hon. A. O. Smoot, and Mr. H. H. Cluff, Mr. Hemenway was installed in the office of the

Provo *Enquirer*, a local semi-weekly newspaper, as an editorial writer. During the next few weeks some original articles made the subscribers of the *Enquirer* rather open their eyes, we suspect. Hemenway was not a Mormon, but the *Enquirer* belonged to a Mormon, and the new editor took delight in defending a people whom he knew were often shamefully abused and villainously misrepresented. The result of his outspoken, frank and vigorous utterances in behalf of the Mormons was gratifying. The great journalistic guns of the anti-Mormons in Salt Lake City began to turn their attention to the *Enquirer* at once, and Mr. John Nicholson, associate editor of the *Deseret News*, wrote to Mr. Hemenway offering him a permanent position at good wages on the Ogden *Daily Herald*. This seemed like a good opportunity to enlarge the sphere of his usefulness, and the stranger editor availed himself of Mr. Nicholson's suggestion. In a few days the president of the Ogden *Herald* Publishing Company, Hon. L. W. Shurtliff, and the business manager, Mr. E. H. Anderson, visited Provo and ratified a contract with Mr. Hemenway, who proceeded to Ogden a week or two later and assumed editorial control of the Ogden Daily and Semi-Weekly *Herald* on the morning of his twenty-fourth birthday, or March 22, 1885. How much success Mr. Hemenway attained in the next four or five months in his new editorial capacity is a matter of history, which is pretty significantly illustrated by the fact that within that brief period the anti-Mormons of Ogden were somewhat demoralized, and did not hesitate to threaten his life, and even attempt to assault him at his place of residence and upon the highways, but a kind of charm seemed to preserve his person from the murderous missiles and weapons of his totally discomfitted opponents. Then the powerful enginery of the law was pitted against him, and a packed grand jury, composed entirely of his enemies, found two indictments against him for libel. His enemies had conceived the brilliant but cowardly scheme of securing his conviction by a trial jury composed exclusively of his most deadly foes. But on the other hand the whole body of the Mormon people for miles around, and many honorable Gentiles, threw around him the sustaining grace of their sympathy and general cordial support, and even the unscrupulous and abandoned malignity of his rankling enemies augmented his strength and stimulated his exertions. They could not silence his tongue with a bribe or fetter his pen with a threat, and he received hundreds of letters applauding his courage and integrity of purpose. Meanwhile the circulation of the Ogden *Herald* continued to increase; its editorials were copied to the advantage of the Mormon people abroad, and it became a considerable local power in politics, business and religious concerns. This result had been attained by the first of July, and Mr. Hemenway deemed himself sufficiently well founded upon the rock of public confidence to command a moderate support for a family. Then, and not till then, did he seek the acquaintance of the young and handsome lady who had inspired all his strenuous exertions for full five months, during which time he had never once heard from her or seen her face, so full of the lustre of beauty to his eyes, but the memory of her amiable features with all their innocence and sunshine was treasured in his heart like the recollection of a holy vision. Should we recount the story of his love conquest? Will the young people of a future day care to read the simple tale? Perhaps not, and yet it is a brief and harmless narrative. The editor turned wooer with all the ardor of his soul. Miss Ireta Dixon was a name that bound him as by magic. He readily secured an introduction to her, but there were other beaux who had, perhaps, already found favor in her eyes, and how could he win her from them? We don't know exactly how he did it, but it was soon his happy fortune to become an accepted lover. Then followed a brief but delightful courtship, with all the glory of moonlight rides and lovers' walks and talks, when the pure emanations of the heart made earth a paradise and life an apt foretaste of immortal and elysian joys. Oh! those were happy days—for an editor; and they will never fade while memory retains her power. And then, on the twenty-ninth of September, 1885, came the wedding day with its train of happiness. Only think, Hemenway won the idol of his heart in three months. You may be sure he was a zealous suitor, and the while he wooed Ireta he continued to hurl the javelins of his criticism among the anti-Mormons, who were in a condition of chronic combustion about half the time as a consequence—but the wooing and the wedding went on just the same. That was the happiest day in all his existence when the young editor led his bride to the altar on that fair September day in Payson. And then the wedding feast was such a home-like, happy one, and the ball in the City Hall so merry and pleasant. And next day, let us not forget the formal parting of the young bride and the associates of her youth, her venerable father and many relatives. It was a touching scene, so full of pathos as to melt the heart in tears. Ah, but what can equal the noble, confiding love and confidence of a young woman, for the first time giving her affections and herself with it to the man she loves! And how shall a man sufficiently appreciate such a precious, PRICELESS gift?

Ireta! as we write this, the clock numbers the hour which completes the first anniversary of our wedding day—September 29, 1886. Is your husband less a lover now than he was ere he espoused you on that bright September day one year ago? Has he not loved you with an equal, truthful love, and cared for you with an ever increasing tenderness and devotion? You know his inmost heart; not one thought that slumbers there but is your own. 'Tis true he is not with you to guard your slumbers, guide your amusements, or help you pass the tedious hours in mirth. A judge—a Federal judge—tore him from you, and threw him into prison for a year, and you are sorrowful and lonely now; your true, warm, woman's heart was wounded and His Honor satisfied. But you do know now, sweet wife, how more than ever dear your faithful husband is to you, and you to him since that judge did his utmost, and ceased to be a judge forever. Thus may it ever be, O wife and husband. Pure and true affection is eternal; age and misfortune but strengthen and exalt it; peace, virtue, honor and long life grow out of it in this world, and merge into it in the eternities to come; therefore, Ireta, how brighter than a star must the happy future be?

CHAPTER XXI.

Some Account of Miss Ireta Dixon and her Family.—Utah Girls make Good Wives.

MISS IRETA DIXON, who became the wife of Charles W. Hemenway on the twenty-ninth day of September, 1885, was born in Bountiful, Davis County, Utah, September 20th, 1866. Her parents sprang from sturdy and famous old Anglo-Saxon families. On her father's side, great-grandfather Dixon was born in Yorkshire, England; his wife was a daughter of the Coats family of thread manufacturing fame. Great-grandfather and mother Dixon emigrated to America in 1758. They settled at the head of the Bay of Fundy, in New Brunswick, upon a small harbor which is known to this day as Dixon's Landing. During the Revolutionary war their eldest son, Charles, was drafted into the British service and stationed at Fort Cumberland, on the Bay of Fundy. He served with distinction through the war. In 1790, he traveled through the United States. He stayed some two months where the city of Cincinnati now stands, but where only a few log cabins were then to be found. Thence he proceeded down to New Orleans, where he remained a few months, and then returned by the way of New York to his parental home in New Brunswick, where he became a farmer and then a ship-builder. Subsequently he sold out and emigrated to what was known as the Western Reserve in Ohio, and located some twenty miles from Cleveland, in 1854. Some years later he set out for Utah, but as the result of an accident he died in Davenport, Iowa. His wife and Ireta's grandmother, Elizabeth Dixon, lived to reach Utah, and died at Payson City, in 1864, having attained her eighty-sixth year.

Edward Dixon, Ireta's father, was born in Sackville, N. B., August 17th, 1818. He emigrated to Ohio with Charles Dixon, his father, in

1837, and in 1844 he visited Hancock County, Illinois, and saw Governor Ford come in with his three thousand men to take the city of Nauvoo. Later on he was present in Carthage at the trial of Sharp and Williams for the murder of Joseph and Hyrum Smith. Then he returned to Ohio, and subsequently emigrated to Portage County, Indiana, where he engaged in farming and stock-raising until 1854, when he drove stock across the plains to California in company with Orrawell Simons, Sr. At the Missouri River, where Mr. Dixon arrived late in the season, it was ascertained that the Indians were menacing emigrants, and after a delay of a few days a party consisting of Squire Hicox, his son Bronson, his daughter Delia, and others from Ohio and Illinois, came along and all proceeded west together for their mutual protection. With some difficulty they crossed the Missouri River about six miles above Council Bluffs, and pushed on to the westward as vigorously as possible, in the hope of overtaking other parties, that all might travel with greater safety. The third day out from the Missouri, a camp of wagons was sighted some distance ahead, but upon examination it was found that the Indians had carried off the stock, cut up the harness and left no trace of the unfortunate emigrants. This illustrates some of the perils of that time, which those who crossed the plains had to encounter. A few days later, Captain Davis and a party from Wisconsin came in sight. The two companies united, for strength and safety. The road was marked by many fresh graves, and stations were deserted. After a variety of more or less startling incidents, Mr. Dixon arrived in Salt Lake Valley September 6th, 1854. After helping to open up the settlement of Spanish Fork, in Utah Valley, whither Mr. Dixon went with Mr. O. Simons and others from Salt Lake Valley, he proceeded on to California with his cattle. In company with others he traveled over three hundred miles towards the Pacific Coast without any unusual trouble, but soon after, near a place called Stony Creek, Indians made a desperate effort to steal some of the cattle and succeeded in getting a number of the animals some distance from camp before they could be overtaken and recovered. Several times the Indians came into camp and were with difficulty placated. Mr. Dixon and party finally arrived in California on the first day of July, 1855. Soon afterwards, he located in the coast range of mountains, and remained there raising stock until 1859, when he visited San Francisco, took passage for Panama on the *Golden Gate*, and thence crossed the isthmus to Aspinwall, and sailed to New York, where he landed on the twenty-sixth of May, 1859. That same year he proceeded to Cleveland, Ohio, and was married to Sarah Gould.

Ireta's great-grandfather on her mother's side was John Gould. He served all through the Revolutionary war in the patriot army. He settled in the State of New York, where he lived until 1812, when he again took up his musket to fight Great Britain. He was a member of a cavalry company, and at the battle of Lundy's Lane he was killed while charging the enemy. His horse was also killed by the same missile that caused his death. By the side of the old Revolutionary hero, when he fell, rode his son, John Gould, Jr. He lived to see the war ended, and became one of the first settlers of Cleveland, Ohio, where his daughter, Sarah, Ireta's mother, was born, February 17th, 1828. There, too, Sarah Gould grew to womanhood, and from there, just after her marriage with Edward Dixon, in 1859, she departed for Indiana and California in the spring of 1860. After the tedious march which such a trip overland involved in those days of hardships and privations, Ireta's parents settled in Lake County, California. Three years later they removed to Napa Valley, and on the third of July, 1865, they came back to Utah by way of the "Pony Express" route. They settled at Bountiful, where we have already learned their daughter, Mrs. Ireta Hemenway, was born. In 1867, Mr. Dixon bought a farm in Farmington, and in June, 1869, Mrs. Dixon, with Ireta, then but three-years old, took the train at Ogden for the east and visited her old home in Ohio. After a month's absence, she returned, and then the family removed to Payson City, in Utah County, where they have resided ever since, and where Ireta's mother died April 18th, 1882. Mr. Edward Dixon still resides in Payson, where he has two daughters, both older than Ireta, and one son, Eddie, who is the youngest of the family. The old gentleman is now venerable with years, but he is well preserved and hearty. His life has been that of a pioneer. In his younger days he was tall and strong, and admirably qualified to contend with the rugged vicissitudes of a pioneer career; and few have toiled harder or labored with better motives than Father Dixon or "Uncle Ed." as he is familiarly called in Payson. His departed wife, who sleeps in the Payson burial grounds, was a helpmate in the truest and best sense. As a mother, she was fond and kind and faithful; as a wife, she was tender and true. Her life latterly was wholly devoted to her children, whom she loved with an unusual affection and tried to rear in the paths of righteousness and honor.

Such, briefly, were the ancestors of the young lady whom Mr. Hemenway has made his wife—a young lady born amid these valleys of the mountains, and overflowing with such good qualities of head and heart that best equip women for the consummation of perfect wifehood. Here in this Mormon Territory also has she always lived. At Brigham Young Academy, at Provo, she obtained educational advantages, and by associations among the peculiar people of this region have her social habits been formed. In all things she is a typical Utah girl—as lovely as any and as brave and true.

CHAPTER XXII.

A Sketch of the Libel Suits.—In Jail.—"Good Bye."

PEOPLE, etc., *vs.* Charles W. Hemenway; libel." This was the title of three cases on the docket of the First District Court of Utah, which were to come up for trial, in Ogden, during the month of December, 1885. The first case was tried. Mr. Hemenway was unable to provide himself with an attorney, and *was therefore compelled to defend himself.* The indictment had been found by a grand jury which had just been severely criticised by the defendant, and the alleged libel consisted in publishing in the Ogden *Herald,* some months before, an editorial in which the opinion was expressed that U. S. Prosecuting Attorney, W. H. Dickson, U. S. Commissioner, Wm. McKay, and other Federal officers were pooling their fees. The editor had based this article upon current report and divers communications. Prior to the time of the alleged libelous publication, he had never met or had any dealings with any of the gentlemen aggrieved. Prior to the time when he was indicted and arrested, he had never been given an opportunity to correct the erroneous publication, as he would gladly have done if his attention had been called to the facts. The alleged libel was published in good faith. The editor was persuaded that his opinion was justified by the reports he had received, and due to the public. He never received any intimation that the article was considered a libel, until he was informed that the grand jury had it under consideration. Wm. McKay, one of the parties who thought he had been libeled, on the witness stand at the trial, swore that the alleged defamatory article did him no harm, but that it perhaps did him some good. Neither he nor any of the other gentlemen, presumably aggrieved, had complained to the grand jury, or asked that Mr. Hemenway be indicted. That august body had acted upon its own motion. It was composed exclusively of anti-Mormons; the parties whom it alleged, by indictment, had been libeled, were eminent anti-Mormons; the trial jury was composed exclusively of anti-Mormon partizans; the judge before whom the case was tried was an anti-Mormon, and the defenseless young defendant had distinguished himself as a journalistic defender of the persecuted Mormon people. The case was conducted on the part of the prosecution by J. L. Rawlins, Esq., a brilliant and eloquent attorney of Salt Lake City, and Mr. Hemenway pleaded his own cause, as best he could, alone. The jury brought in a verdict of "guilty," as a matter of course. Mr. Hemenway, under oath, frankly acknowledged the publication, and under the libel law of Utah, which presumes malice, no doubt he was technically guilty. Under the same law, every other newspaper editor in the Territory might probably be convicted from one to a thousand times, with a hostile judge and jury, and especially with no means of securing a proper legal defense. But the utmost efforts of the prosecution failed to show that Mr. Hemenway had been actuated in the publication of the libel by the least actual personal malice.

The next day, the other two cases against Mr. Hemenway were set for trial. One of these was an alleged libel on General Nathan Kimball, of Ogden. In this case the aggrieved gentleman entered complaint against Mr. Hemenway for criminal prosecution, and also sued him and the Ogden *Herald* Company conjointly for $20,000 damages. The editorial complained of had been published by the editor a month or two after he assumed control of the Ogden *Herald*. Among other things the libel consisted in the statement that the impecuniosity of the prosecuting witness, General Kimball, rendered him susceptible to corruption, a hasty statement which the *Deseret News* disapproved, and which no one regretted more than the defendant himself after he became acquainted with the General. Prior to the publication of the attack upon Mr. Kimball, Mr. Hemenway had never been introduced to him nor had any dealings with him. Consequently there could have been no actual personal malice in the premises.

In publishing the alleged defamatory article in this case, Mr. Hemenway was of necessity relying upon the statements of others, believing that he was uttering the truth, and as the General was foreman of the then grand jury in the First Judicial District of Utah, his character as a public servant in that capacity was of course open to public criticism.

The final libel case pending at this time against Editor Hemenway was instigated by the grand jury. The party whom the defendant was accused of libeling in this instance was none other than Hon. Charles S. Zane, Chief Justice of Utah. Mr. Zane did not complain in this case. In fact we are informed that the honorable gentleman declares he has never yet read the alleged defamation of his character for which the author is now undergoing one year's imprisonment. This alleged libel was written in a period of much local excitement. Among other things the Chief Justice was charged with rendering a crooked decision in a certain case growing out of the sensational revelations in connection with the matter that led to the imprisonment of Mr. B. Y. Hampton for conspiracy. As soon as Mr. Hemenway was made aware that his article in this case was considered libelous, he hastened to explain that he meant that His Honor had rendered a crooked decision in accord with a crooked law. The editor further practically apologized in print by disclaiming the intention of uttering even a disrespectful word concerning the Chief Justice. Nevertheless, Mr. Hemenway was promptly indicted, although Mr. Zane entered no complaint. The editor seemed to be looked upon as a shining mark for prosecution because he was trying to defend an unpopular people, but more especially because he was poor and defenseless, and so entirely a stranger that he was compelled to rely upon reports and statements obtained from others.

When the Kimball and Zane libels came up for trial, Mr. Hemenway found himself entirely exhausted by his labors to defend himself singlehanded during his trial for libel the day before, and moreover he despaired of a successful defense because of the partizan leanings of the court and entire jury panel that were to try him, and also because of the unqualified presumption of malice according to the law against libel. For these and other reasons, he withdrew his former pleas of "not guilty," and pleaded "guilty" in both the Zane and Kimball cases. The court, of its own motion, then suspended sentence for a month in all three cases. In the meanwhile, as always before, through the columns of the Ogden *Herald* Mr. Hemenway expressed a desire to keep strictly within the limits of the law concerning libel. The Mormon people did not want any improper weapons, such as libel or slander, used even against a libelous or slanderous enemy. And Mr. Hemenway was the last person in the world to desire to assail worthy gentlemen unjustly. But at the same time, as a public journalist, he desired to do his duty fearlessly in exposing corruption in official quarters. Necessarily he was compelled to write from the information with which he was supplied because he was a stranger in a strange land, and moreover no editor can by any possibility hunt up proof to substantiate every apparently reliable report that he receives, upon the same day when it must be published or rejected and killed as news.

When, in January, 1886, Mr. Hemenway again appeared in court for sentence, he was surprised to be greeted with marked courtesy, by the presiding judge, who, in the case of the first alleged libel upon Messrs. Dickson, *et al.*, imposed a fine of $200.00 and costs, and in the other two cases, suspended sentence indefinitely, *not during good behavior*. The fine and costs in this case were promptly paid by public contributions ranging from ten cents to ten dollars, and coming from all classes of people in Ogden, and throughout the surrounding territory. By some of the donors to Mr. Hemenway's relief, the editor was looked upon as the innocent victim of circumstances, and others politically opposed, such as Fred. J. Keisel & Co., who contributed $2.50, exercised their generosity in his behalf, with purely charitable motives to save the editor from imprisonment, although they by no means approved his editorial course.

Afterwards, Mr. Hemenway continued to edit the Ogden *Herald* until the twenty-ninth day of July, 1886, when he was suddenly called before the United States court, at Ogden, and asked to show cause why sentence in the cases suspended over him should not then be passed upon him. On the part of the prosecution, Ogden Hiles, Esq., stated that his attention had been called to the record, which showed that the order of the Court suspending sentence in these cases, had been improvidently made, and he moved that the Court should consider the matter. On the part of Mr. Hemenway, J. N. Kimball, Esq., made an eloquent plea for the fair treatment of the defendant. Then the Judge, with some asperity, fined the editor $500.00 in the Kimball case, and sentenced him to one year's imprisonment in Weber County Jail for the Zane libel. His Honor refused to admit the editor to bail pending appeal, and ordered him into the custody of the U. S. Marshal, until the fine was paid. Mr. Hemenway was saved from the Marshal's custody through the courtesy of Mr. Warren G. Childs, Sr., and Mr. Edward H. Anderson, who advanced him the money to pay the $500 fine, on his note. Then the prisoner was turned over to the custody of the Sheriff of Weber County and consigned to jail.

Soon after Mr. Hemenway had pleaded "guilty" to the criminal charge of libeling General Kimball, the civil suit against him and the Ogden *Herald* Company for $20,000 was compromised upon the confession of judgment for $500 by the defendants. Thus it was after this settlement that the court fined the editor $500 more for the same offense.

The imposition of final sentence upon Mr. Hemenway in these cases was about the last official act of the then judge of the First District Court of Utah. The United States Senate for cause had failed to confirm his nomination to the judgeship, and President Cleveland had withdrawn his name and presented that of Hon. H. P. Henderson, of Michigan, instead.

It must be remembered that the now ex-judge who sentenced the editor so peculiarly, had more than once, especially about that time, trembled under the editor's criticisms. Mr. Hemenway had opposed his confirmation by the Senate, and sharply animadverted upon the eccentricities of his judicial conduct. Among the charges which had been preferred against him were the allegations of Hon. P. H. Emerson, for twelve years Associate Justice of the Supreme Court of Utah, to the effect that the now ex-judge was vindictive, and that he had applied to learned and honorable members of the Utah bar, such as Judges Sutherland and Emerson, profanely abusive epithets like "G—d d—d skunks." A few days after this judicial fellow imposed sentence upon the editor, for reasons best known to himself, he left the Territory for Michigan, and went back into obscurity, from which he ought never to have emerged in the first place.

Mr. Hemenway went to prison with all possible good grace, but he was grieved exceedingly on account of his young and tender wife. To her the sudden and unexpected announcement of her husband's sentence came like a stroke of lightning, smiting her affectionate heart with anguish and sorrow inexpressible. Yet did she soon recover from the first shock of the event, and bear up nobly and bravely under the cloud of pain as only a faithful, true and courageous wife and sweetheart can. Although her health was then delicate, she soon dashed away the burning tears and sought with all her soul to comfort her incarcerated companion, and from that first sad hour to the time of his release three letters passed between them every day. Up to the hour of the husband's incarceration, their life together had been one continual honeymoon, which—they hope that you, kind reader, will not be surprised to learn—they trust and believe will last while they both live, and be renewed to continue forever in brighter realms where libels will never be inadvertantly uttered or vindictively and cruelly avenged.

The following communication, published in the Ogden *Herald* of August 7th, 1886, gives some idea how the incarcerated editor passed the first seven days in jail:

Editor Herald:

It is a source of unalloyed gratification to be able to communicate with my old friends through the columns of your paper once again. From the many inquiries respecting my condition and sentiments, which have been made since my incarceration, I am happy to feel sure that I yet hold a kindly interest in the hearts of an ever-generous and lenient upright public. It is, therefore, with a measure of genuine pleasure that I once again address myself, as your correspondent, to the people of Ogden and all the readers of the Ogden *Herald*, with a view to acquaint them with my present situation and those feelings which arise from my deprivation of liberty by the order of the First District Court.

Since efficient and dutiful Sheriff Belnap, in obedience to the dictates of his duty, conducted me to the basement of the Court House, in Ogden, and initiated me into the mysteries of Weber County Jail for the first time, I have been imprisoned nine days. Seven-ninths of that time have been passed in the dark and dreary dungeons which compose Weber County Jail, but which are nevertheless secure and proper places for the confinement of desperate criminals. Those seven days dragged their slow length along tediously indeed. It matters not how clear a conscience a prisoner may have, he must be a very hard and abandoned character, indeed, not to have some cause to bemoan the loss of his liberty, but I had something more to weep for.

The general reader of the local papers will doubtless remember some partisan controversy occasioned by O. W. Powers' presentation of a set of silver spoons as a wedding present to my wife on the occasion of our marriage in Payson just ten months to a day prior to my consignment to jail by his ex-Honor. Well, when I got snugly ensconced in confinement, my mind wandered back to that happiest of days when I espoused the first woman that I ever really loved. Again in imagination my youthful bride stood before me in all her wedding regalia and the beauty of diffident maidenhood. Again I see the ceremony which united our hands and our hearts. Again the wedding guests extend their hearty congratulations and marriage bells of mirth and music echo on my ears, in fancy. And then the festive company assemble around the bounteously laden tables, and the wedding cake is cut. Peals of laughter, repartee and gaiety mingle in a very symphony of joy, and smiles illumine every face. And later the dance claims every heart. But when the ball is over and the guests have retired, an aged father brings forth a mysterious missive received by post, and directed: "Mrs. C. W. Hemenway, Payson, Utah." The dainty letter is opened in the presence of the bride and groom, and it reads as follows:

"*Miss Ireta Dixon:*

"Accept my most cordial congratulations and best wishes. I send a slight token of my respect by express.
"O W. POWERS."

* * * * * * * *

Awakening with a start, I glared at my prison walls, which were faintly outlined by an uncertain light. It was the first morning of my imprisonment, and—reader, I had been dreaming. I can't begin to tell all the thoughts that surged through my mind at that moment of waking. The hours that immediately followed seemed to me an eternity of torment, and I would have given my right arm or the best ten years of my life and never edited a paper again this side of that bourne whence no traveler returns, if I could have returned to solace and attend the one whom I live for.

I suppose I am a peculiar being for a man twenty-six years of age. Perhaps I am a solecism among mankind, but I had rather suffer a thousand degrees of agony than be the source or cause of a single pang inflicted upon another uselessly and deliberately. This is why I shrink from imprisonment. As for myself, I defy the utmost shafts of punishment or torture if they are only confined to me. Have I not borne patiently and without murmuring the bitterest shafts of criticism? Have I ever sought to exact the "pound of flesh" nominated in the bond? Have I not forgiven my enemies and blessed those that cursed me?

For the last two days I have occupied new quarters. Sheriff Belnap, responding to what seemed to be a general public opinion, fitted up an additional compartment appended to the county jail, which he has had in contemplation since long before my incarceration; and which is much pleasanter and more cheerful than my former jail lodgings. This compartment I occupy. It is on the first floor of the Court House building, in the northwest corner thereof, and there I shall be very happy to see my friends at proper times when the Sheriff will permit.

I have to acknowledge with gratitude many gifts that enhance the meagre comforts of my situation, and thank heaven that my circumstances are not as bad as they might be by any means.

CHAS. W. HEMENWAY.

OGDEN JAIL, Aug. 7, 1886.

CHAPTER XXIII.

About the Mormons.—The Wonderful Religion of the Latter-day Saints.

EVERYBODY has heard of the Mormons, but people generally, outside of Utah and immediately adjoining localities, know very little that is really true about them. The people commonly called Mormons denominate themselves the Church of Jesus Christ of Latter-day Saints. They number over two hundred thousand souls, and the present seat of their power is Salt Lake City, Utah. The religion of the Mormons is based upon the Bible, and upon the revelations of Joseph Smith, whom they esteem a prophet ordained by the living God of Abraham, Isaac and Jacob to inaugurate the dispensation of the fulness of times, and prepare the way for the second advent of Christ and the millennium as foretold in the Scriptures. Joseph Smith claimed, and the Mormons believe that he received visits from angels, and that the keys to the ancient lost Priesthood of God were restored to him. As we understand it, the Priesthood represents the authority of the Almighty on earth, and the keys of this authority are presumed to be in direct communion with God. Joseph Smith held the keys to this august authority while he lived. His first successor to this power was the celebrated Brigham Young, and the venerable John Taylor now stands at the head of the Mormon Church, and holds the keys of the Priesthood as prophet, seer and revelator. The "Book of Mormon" purports to be a divinely authentic history which Joseph Smith translated from gold plates discovered hidden in the hill Cumorah, in New York State, where Joseph was directed to find them by an angel. This book does not in any sense supersede the Bible in the estimation of the Mormons. "The Doctrine and Covenants," and the revelations of Joseph Smith are, we understand, regarded as quite as authoritative as the Bible. The Mormon prophet was born in Vermont, in 1805. He organized what is now known as the Mormon Church in 1830. He taught his followers the principle of gathering together to live in one locality, and Kirtland, Ohio, Jackson County, Missouri, and Nauvoo, Illinois, were successively the centre of their gathering. In 1844, at Carthage, near Nauvoo, Joseph was brutally murdered by a mob, and his successor, Brigham Young, subsequently led the Mormons across the plains to Utah, which was a barren, mountainous wilderness when the pioneers first entered Salt Lake Valley, July 24, 1847. After enduring fearful hardships, with the lapse of a few years an era of prosperity and peace came to the exiled and sequestered Mormons. By industry and frugality, they have overcome the natural sterility of the country, and according to the common saying "made it blossom as the rose." It is not our purpose to dwell further upon the history of the Mormons. This we have written by way of introduction for the benefit of the unacquainted reader.

When Charles W. Hemenway came to Utah, in January, 1885, he had an ardent curiosity to obtain an inside view of Mormon character and Mormon institutions. From experience he had learned that the best way to measure the merits or defects of a particular people was to mingle familiarly with the masses. This he soon began to do, in spite of formidable obstacles, as we have seen, at Payson, in Utah County. He found the people generally unquestionably sincere in their religious views, and emphatically in earnest to carry out only what they conscientiously believed to be the design and will of God. They were virtuous, temperate, industrious and honest, peaceful and law-abiding, as a rule. Nearly every male adult in good standing in the Church held office in the Priesthood, the keys of which were held by John Taylor, the President of the Church and the living Prophet of the Lord. Next in authority to the President and his two counselors, Hons. George Q. Cannon and Joseph F. Smith, a son of Hyrum Smith, the Prophet Joseph's brother, were the Twelve Apostles. Under them were quorums of Seventies, Presidencies of Stakes, Bishops, Teachers, Home Missionaries and Elders, comprising nearly the entire adult male membership of the Church, all organized in superb subordination and efficiency. To the chief of these authorities (all holding varying degrees of power solely by virtue of their rank in the Priesthood) the people looked with respect as to the representative of God on earth. The masses of the Mormon people felt that the laws of the Almighty were paramount to the laws of men, and as a natural consequence paid higher allegiance and greater homage to those who were representatives and executors of the Divine laws, by virtue of their high Priesthood, than they could to the agents and executors of men's laws. Nevertheless they scrupulously observed, as a rule, all of the wholesome and usual laws of the civil and criminal code of the Territory. The Church government was in the hands of the Priesthood, at the head of which stood John Taylor, in chief authority, with his counselors, the Twelve Apostles, Seventies and Presidents of Stakes, Bishops in subordinate control, like the general of an army with his aids and subordinate commanders. The Church contemplated the entire temporal and spiritual government of its members. It had its own courts and judiciary, with President Taylor at the head to try offenses against the Church, leaving members amenable to the law of the land when that was broken by them. The Church owned much property, and each member was expected to pay into its treasury one-tenth of his or her annual income, all of which was at the disposition of the President, as Trustee-in-Trust for the Church, who, without bonds or sureties, appeared to be considered accountable to God alone. The doctrines of the Church inculcate honesty, virtue, frugality, devotion, humility, obedience to authority, hospitality and industry, and discourage evil generally. The Mormon religion is a scheme for the redemption of mankind from the consequences of sin, just the same as other religous systems are. Its particular mission is, however, to prepare the way for the second advent of Christ and the millennium. It claims to be a restoration of the primitive and original religion of Jesus and of the Bible. The most preposterous, wild and sensational ideas respecting Mormonism, or the faith of the Latter-day Saints of Utah, prevail in the world at large. In order to be understood thoroughly, fairly, or anything like perfectly, the whole Mormon system must be diligently and candidly studied for a long time. It is a great fabric, in many respects totally unlike any religious system now upon the earth, and in order to be properly understood it must be studied from the standard Mormon works on theology and history, such as the Doctrine and Covenants, the Book of Mormon, the Pearl of Great Price, the Voice of Warning, the History of the Mormon Battalion, The Martyrs, Spencer's Letters, Journal of Discourses, Martyrdom of Joseph Standing, and many other publications which are authoritative and especially valuable to the student of the genius of Mormon institutions. For the benefit of the stranger who may be curious to investigate the most remarkable religious phenomena of the nineteenth century, we will say that the above and all other authentic Mormon Church works may be procured of Abram H. Cannon, Ogden, Utah, or of Cannon & Sons or The *Deseret News* Company, Salt Lake City. Although the writer has been in Utah nearly two years, and has enjoyed exceptional opportunities of forming a correct opinion of the Mormon creed, he has not by any means mastered all its principles. Two-thirds—nay, ninety-nine one-hundredths of the ordinary books about Utah and the Mormons, written by transient visitors or speculative politicians, are utterly worthless, full of the most stupid absurdities and extravaganzas. The transient visitor to Salt Lake is generally seized upon by politicians who have an object in view, and for various purposes mislead the enquirer. Even the older and more intelligent residents of Utah are as a rule rarely well qualified to enlighten the stranger fairly to any extent, concerning the realities of Mormondom. This much we say by way of cautioning the enquirer after truth. For whether we regard Mormonism as a fraud or as an inspired and holy religious system, it is eminently worthy of investigation equally by the scholar, the philosopher, the statesman, the publicist, or the honest farmer and general reader, because it embraces or stands upon a grand and almost marvelous organization which has defied all opposition, and continued to grow strong for more than half a century, and which offers to redeem the world from all the social, political and ethical troubles of the times, and lead humanity, as in one harmonious family, back under the perfect government of God. Whatever your faith may be, whether you call yourself a Methodist, a Baptist, a Presbyterian, an infidel, an anarchist, or what not, thoughtful reader, you will find it both pleasant and profitable to study Mormonism from the standard authorized publications of the Mormon Church, but most books that profess to give an idea of either the Mormons or their religion are, as a rule, very little better than stale and stupid fictions.

CHAPTER XXIV.

Plural Marriage.—Miscellaneous.—Scenery.—Railroads.— Mining Resources.

THE Mormons generally are not a luxurious, proud or boastful people; neither are they vain-glorious, egotistical or haughty. They are rather simple, plain and straightforward. They deprecate all luxury, and appreciate a manly hardihood which prevails among them. They maintain remarkably fraternal relations among themselves. They care for each other, and there are no real paupers or beggars among them. All are frugal in their habits of living, economical and charitable. Hospitality is a special feature of their faith, and they are safe as debtors, accommodating as neighbors, and generally full of the milk of human kindness, as is exemplified by their numerous charitable and other liberal donations for the benefit of humanity. It may not be generally known that the Mormon preachers or teachers of the Gospel receive no salaries; all or any members of the Priesthood are liable to be called from the audience to preach at any time. The office of a Mormon Bishop is not so important, relatively, as the bishop's office in other churches. A Mormon Bishop simply presides over a Ward or precinct. All Utah and that portion of adjoining Territories occupied by the Saints are subdivided into ecclesiastical Wards; the Wards in each county generally are combined into an ecclesiastical division called a Stake of Zion, over which a President and two Counselors preside. Every adult male Mormon is liable to serve as a missionary for two or more years, subject to a call from the First Presidency of the Church. Many Latter-day Saints fill two, three and four two-year missions. In fact, as we understand the matter, every Mormon in good standing is supposed to hold himself ready to obey all calls made in the name of his religion and his God, through the First Presidency or the proper subordinate authority.

The Mormons believe in baptism for the dead, and have erected and are erecting magnificent temples wherein to formally make covenants with their God and each other, and to perform the various ordinances of their faith both for the living and the dead. Their temples are sacred structures. There is one at St. George, in southern Utah, and one in the northern part of the Territory at Logan, while a grand one has been in course of construction for years in Salt Lake City, and yet it is not finished. A fourth temple is also in course of construction at Manti, in Sanpete County. All these temples are or will be noble structures, built to endure the vicissitudes of time, and furnished with a magnificence becoming an august sanctuary of the Most High. Formerly in what is known as the Endowment House, in Salt Lake City, but latterly within the temples, plural marriages are solemnized. What the world calls polygamy the Mormons call plural or celestial marriage. It is well known that the Mormons believe that it is not only right and proper, but that under certain conditions it is obligatory for one man to have more than one wife at a given time. The Saints believe, too, that a marriage performed by one having authority becomes an eternal bond, and that exaltation and the highest degree of glory in the heavens are dependent in a measure upon the union of men and women in marriage upon earth, and upon the number and faithfulness of their progeny. Not every male Mormon is expected or required to take unto himself many consorts. Plurality of wives is supposed to be reserved for those Saints who, by lives of more perfect purity and faith, make themselves worthy of enjoying the highest confidence. The Mormon people do not approve plural marriage because of a love of lust. They condemn lechery either in or out of the marriage relation most severely and unsparingly. They even hold that sexual intercourse should be restricted to the sole purpose of propagating the species, and the man who marries many women is expected to connubiate with them as a husband only for the object of procreation. They religiously regard the mother of many children as hallowed in a high degree, and they likewise hold the father of many sons and daughters as therefore highly honorable. Their plural marriages are contracted, as they most solemnly believe, for time and eternity, and are professedly entered into for purposes quite the reverse of lust, as a pure matter of religious duty, according to a command of God given through their prophet, Joseph.

Mormon plural marriage cannot be fairly compared with Mohammedan or Asiatic polygamy. In practice the Mormon system of plurality has nothing in common with oriental plurality. Plural wives of the Latter-day Saints are not shut up in harems, but they are allowed every liberty, and assigned a high and responsible position as the conductors of a family, and the supports of a home, after fashion of the American type. Generally speaking we have found that the polygamists of Utah are the brightest, strongest and most admirable of all the Mormon people, both in an intellectual and a physical sense. Our observation also proves that the offspring of plural marriages among the Mormons are by no means inferior to the issue of monogamous wedlock.

As a consequence of the unmolested practice of polygamy in Utah for many years, we find the leading or older families of the Territory extremely numerous, and generally closely related through marriage. We take it that this in great part accounts for the wonderful fraternity which exists among the Saints, and their union upon all questions affecting them as a body. The whole

Mormon community is bound together by a cordial unity of sentiment, belief and interest, which is especially remarkable in this age of individual aggression, when every man's hand throughout the world at large seems uplifted against his fellow-being.

Among themselves the Mormons have introduced an excellent system of co-operation in manufacturing enterprises and business generally. In many settlements throughout Utah there is a co-operative store which the people own and control, and which retails all sorts of legitimate merchandise. Zion's Co-operative Mercantile Institution, of Salt Lake, is a great and successful wholesale and retail concern, with a large branch house at Ogden. All of these co-operative institutions are worthy monuments of Mormon thrift and business prudence. Moreover, the principles of co-operation, which the Mormons adhere to, are a decided advance towards the solution of the general contest between capital and labor.

As a rule the Mormons own their own homes, and the land they cultivate. They liberally support non-sectarian public schools, and, considering the comparative newness of the Territory, the schools of Utah are creditable in the extreme.

Outside of Salt Lake, Ogden, Logan and Provo cities, the people generally reside in small towns, where dram-shops and bawdy-houses are conspicuous by their absence, and where quiet, thrift and peace, and harmony and plenty are always to be found.

In the matter of grand and imposing scenery Utah has few equals in all the world. The Territory embraces a considerable extent of lofty mountains. Only the valleys of limited area are susceptible of cultivation by the aid of irrigation. Great Salt Lake, famous as the Dead Sea of America, is in the midst of a mammoth basin right in the backbone of the American continent. Upon the east and west, Salt Lake Valley and Salt Lake at a distance are enfiladed by lofty mountains, whose brows are covered with snow during many months of the year. The climate in this wonderful region is mild, healthful and usually delightful, and it would be hard to find a more inviting country for the tourist or health-seeker. Between Denver, Colorado, and the chief cities of Utah, connecting with the Southern Pacific at Ogden, extends the Denver & Rio Grande Railway, an elegantly and thoroughly well equipped road, running through some of the most beautiful, wild, sublime and grotesque scenery. From

Omaha the celebrated Union Pacific Railroad runs through by another equally atttactive route to Ogden, where its branches connect and extend south almost the entire length of the Territory, and north through Idaho into Montana. Completing the great transcontinental line from Omaha to the Pacific Coast, the Southern Pacific Railway connects Ogden with San Francisco, and offers many inducements to the traveler and sight-seer. Ogden City thus occupies the position of a great railroad centre. It contains some seven or eight thousand inhabitants, is growing rapidly, sits in a pleasant locality at the foot of the Wasatch mountains, near the confluence of Weber and Ogden rivers, and the majestic canyons of the same name. At a little distance southwest of the city, glistens the waters of Great Salt Lake, and north and west of the place extends a beautiful, large and fertile tract of valley land. Ogden has ample and first-class hotel accommodations, and it is only a few hours' ride on the Utah Northern to Logan, where a completed, large, massive Mormon temple raises its turrets high towards the heavens. Ogden is the commercial key to Utah, and offers unbounded opportunities to capital and enterprise. The rich and apparently exhaustless mineral resources of the Territory are as yet only in the infancy of their development, and gold and silver ore have been discovered in the neighborhood of Ogden, while but a little distance from the city, up in the Wasatch mountains, the famous Ontario mine is located. Let the stranger visiting Utah be sure to stop at Ogden and drive up through both the neighboring grand canyons; or, if he has an eye to business, let him survey the multiform inducement which Ogden offers; she is destined to be the great commercial entrepot of this vast intermountain region; or, if he is socially inclined and desirous of observing the conditions of life in Mormondom, let him mingle with the typical residents of Ogden.

CHAPTER XXV.

The Mormon Problem.—Utah Courts. Open Venire.—The Crusade.

ONE of the greatest of all the masters of statescraft that ever lived in ancient times, declared that no government, which did not assume to control both the religion and the marriage relations of its subjects, could long survive. The non-Mormons or Gentiles of Utah practically, though perhaps unconsciously, accept this declaration as a fact in the nature of things governmental. It is well known that the Catholic church has and does claim that marriage is a holy sacrament which of right belongs to ecclesiastical rather than civil administration. As we view it, the Mormon Church practically makes the same claim, and the Constitution of the United States seems to have been designed with a view of exempting ecclesiastical affairs from civil jurisdiction. But in our opinion, this constitutional and much vaunted divorce of church and state is rather apparent than real. Throughout the Union, the clergy of the different denominations are a public factor which no statesmen could safely ignore and hope to prosper. The Mormon Church makes no greater claim to specific ecclesiastical jurisdiction over marriage and over the management of its membership than the Catholic church has made in the past, and, more or less covertly, still makes at the present time. Of course the two churches differ widely in their doctrines and dogmas, but the principles upon which each claims authority and specific powers are, to our mind, identical. The Mormon people profess to pay supreme allegiance to the authority and will of God, as interpreted through their prophets and leaders; they are taught and believe that the Constitution of the Union was inspired by the Almighty; their religion obligates them to be loyal to their country and to "render unto Cæsar the things which are Cæsar's," but they maintain that when the laws of men come in contact with what they individually and collectively know to be the law of God, the divine statute is paramount and must be first respected. It is in part because God, represented by the Priesthood, is thus placed above our government by the Mormons, that the Gentiles or anti-Mormons of Utah call them traitors, aliens and rebels. The popular conviction or prejudice against polygamy, of course, attaches to the plural or celestial marriage of the Mormons, and the celebrated Edmunds law providing a penalty of fine and imprisonment for polygamy, and the act of living in a polygamous condition, or cohabiting with more than one woman, which was passed by Congress in 1882, is the latest embodiment of popular sentiment against a plurality of wives. As the Mormons honestly maintain plural marriage as a part of their religious belief, based upon a command of God, which they can only gnore at the peril of their eternal salvation and celestial exaltation, they prefer to suffer the penalties imposed by the most radical execution of the Edmunds law, rather than abandon their plural system, repudiate and desert aged consorts, and violate their most solemn religious contracts and sacred covenants. The Mormons, therefore, insist upon obeying what is sincerely considered to be the law of God, while the Gentiles of Utah, particularly, insist upon the supremacy of the laws of Congress relating to polygamy and unlawful cohabitation. The motives of those who uphold the Edmunds law are various; but few, if any, of its Utah supporters pretend to be actuated by motives of abstract public morality, while the majority profess to uphold the law out of a regard to loyalty to the old flag, but in reality the motive of all is to destroy the political and ecclesiastical autonomy of the Mormon people, and thus to dominate the material and political affairs of the rich Territory. It must be remembered that the Gentiles or non-Mormons of Utah form a very small minority of the citizens of the Territory, and of course they share the fate common to all minorities in a republic, and are through the political union of the Mormons, which they cannot destroy by argument or persuasion, debarred from participating in the local

Territorial government. But at the same time they have a monopoly of all the Federal offices in Utah, which ought to satisfy them, the Mormons very reasonably think. The Federal courts of the Territory are exclusively in the hands of the opponents of the Mormons, and these courts have general jurisdiction in all criminal and civil cases beyond or within the reach of the police courts. All, or nearly all of the jury panels by an open *venire* system are filled deliberately and purposely exclusively from among the known opponents of the Mormons; so the Latter-day Saints plausibly maintain that the judiciary of the Territory is to that extent a mere partisan engine. This circumstance has undoubtedly brought the Federal courts into contempt among the masses. The various interpretations and apparently conflicting constructions put upon the meaning of the law against cohabitation, by different Federal judges, who have taken pains to make their hostility to the Mormons conspicuous, has confirmed this popular contempt, and away down deep in the hearts of the people generally, is the profound conviction that a Mormon can obtain little or no justice under the laws claimed to be so palpably prostituted by an avowedly and practically partisan judicial administration.

Almost invariably the prosecution of Mormons, charged with polygamy and unlawful cohabitation, is made upon the naturally reluctant testimony of the loving wives and children of the alleged offenders. Recently, in the course of a trial in Provo, before the First District Court, the plural wife of the defendant, accused of unlawful cohabitation, was placed upon the witness stand and asked to give the testimony necessary to send her beloved husband to prison. At first she refused to testify, but her accused husband was permitted to persuade her to comply with the order of the court, and then, in her endeavor to answer the fatal questions, she broke entirely down, and the prosecuting attorney was obliged to excuse her temporarily. She left the witness stand with hot tears coursing from her eyes in a convulsion of grief. In this class of cases similar scenes are of frequent occurrence, and they appeal strongly to the humane sentiments of mankind in favor of the accused, and against the wisdom of the law.

Up to the present time in the neighborhood of two hundred Mormons have been convicted of unlawful cohabitation, and some seven or eight of polygamy. The extreme penalty for cohabitation is six months' imprisonment and $300 fine, but the courts have so interpreted the law that a Mormon who has lived with more than one wife continuously for a year or more, may be indicted for each day or other distinct interval of time, and upon each indictment fined and imprisoned to the utmost extent of the law. This makes the penalty in such cases dependent wholly upon the whim of the prosecution, and the man who has continuously cohabited with plural wives for a year might be imprisoned a whole lifetime for the offense. The most of those who have been convicted for unlawful cohabitation are old men about ready to totter into the grave, who formed their plural relations a generation or more ago, before there was any operative law against polygamy. The wives of these venerable men are in many cases in their second infancy, and it seems cruel and useless to disrupt their households by imprisonment. The prosecuting attorney and the courts offer immunity from punishment to all Mormons convicted of unlawful cohabitation if they will promise to obey the Edmunds law in the future, but as this promise involves a repudiation of faithful wives, who have, in most cases, borne the accused husband a family of children, it is deemed unmanly and dishonorable to make it, and moreover such a promise is looked upon as disregardful of God's requirements. Under these circumstances only about six or eight victims of the Edmunds law have purchased immunity from imprisonment by promises; in other words, not one in twenty of the Mormons convicted of polygamy or unlawful cohabitation will pledge themselves to comply in the future with a law which they regard as utterly vicious; nineteen out of twenty will suffer imprisonment and would probably even forfeit life itself rather than be recreant to what they so sincerely and conscientiously consider to be a religious and a manly duty. Yet this refusal to promise obedience to the law against plural relations does not mean that of the Mormons convicted nearly all intend to violate the law deliberately in the future; as a rule men convicted of unlawful cohabitation intend to pay due deference to the law as long as it remains a law, but they merely refuse the Edmunds enactment, deemed so unjust and cruel, the indorsement which a promise would imply, and at the same time reserve to themselves the right to support their plural families and obey what are held to be the commands of God. As a rule, those Mormons who have suffered imprisonment for or been accused of polygamy and unlawful cohabitation are men noted for their fair dealing, integrity, and general law-abiding, thrifty and temperate character. In everything they have been good citizens, and lived exemplary lives without ever having been called into court to defend themselves against any charge whatsoever, except the practice of plural marriage in obedience to an undoubted conscientious conviction, but in violation of a law sincerely believed to be wicked, unconstitutional, and in diametrical opposition to the express fiat of the Almighty.

CHAPTER XXVI.

Three Souls with but a Single Thought; *Three* Hearts that beat as one.

THE Utah enemies of Mormon plural or celestial marriage, base their opposition to that style of matrimony upon a variety of grounds. They say that polygamy degrades womanhood; invites to beastlike indulgence in sexual pleasures, and breaks the hearts of first wives and others, as they are supplanted by new brides; that, moreover, polygamy is a nasty and immoral relic of barbarism, and that in Utah it is the cement of an alien, oriental, combined religious and political system. The average reader, accustomed to monogamic surroundings, is very apt to accept these declarations as true, self-evidently and necessarily. Then follows the impression that the Mormons are indeed a set of monsters. If, however, the reader has had a cosmopolitan experience, or will pause to study what is to him an unknown matter, he will modify his views. The Mormons, generally, do not believe that plural marriage degrades womanhood; they candidly and earnestly believe that the *contrary* is the case. Only men who live exceptionally pure lives, and have attained a degree of good standing in the Church, and are otherwise generally well qualified to perform the duties of a husband and father, are presumed to be allowed to enter the holy order of celestial marriage. The Mormon doctrine and ecclesiastical laws concerning marriage are noteworthy, because they would, if strictly carried out, remove the stigma of sensuality from the plural relationship. In the first place, it must be remembered the Mormons hold that marriage, properly solemnized between competent parties, is eternal; that the great object of matrimony is a propagation of the species; that sexual intercourse must be indulged only for purposes of procreation; that no married man shall take a second or plural wife without the free consent of the first, nor a third without the consent of the first two, and so on; that exaltation in the world to come depends, in a considerable measure, upon the number of the members of a man's household in this world, and that unmarried adults who go in a single state to the next world, no matter how pure their lives may have been on earth, will be deprived of their chief celestial glory, and be reduced to the position of servants or ministering angels of those who, by marriage, have fulfilled a better destiny in their mundane career. All of these propositions are thoroughly believed by the Mormons, and the result is that a plurality of wives or celestial marriage is redeemed from its usual character in theory at least, and surrounded by the halo of sanguine and lofty faith. This, the Mormons claim, is the rule in practice, and our observation confirms it. But there are exceptions to this rule. We could name first wives that have died of broken hearts because their husbands took other consorts, and then, in violation of their covenants with God and the laws of plural union, neglected or even abused the first wife, while the last one was overwhelmed with attentions. We also know of one or two cases in several hundred that have come to our notice, where the professed Mormon has taken several wives through motives of lust, but these cases are rare indeed. The frequent allegation that plural marriage is a nasty and immoral relic of barbarism is not necessarily true. To the pure, all things are pure. Wives of polygamists in Utah are not shut up in harems, but they are given the utmost freedom; the ballot was placed in their hands, and in performing their duties in a plural household they usually acquire a remarkable degree of independence, healthy hardihood and wifely prudence. As mothers, they are wondrously prolific, and their children are generally healthful and hardy. Sexual relations are not immoral in themselves; it is the circumstances that surround intercourse between the sexes, which give moral or immoral color to the relationship. The rights and honors of plural wifehood among the Mormons are made identical with those of monogamous wifehood. The obligations of a polygamist to all his wives are equally sacred; he must provide for each one and care for the children of each; he must also love, honor and cherish each, and all these duties and obligations are lived up to the more scrupulously from the fact that he earnestly believes his household and marital relations will be eternal, if he is faithful to the end. That plural marriage is the cement which holds together the fabric of Mormonism, is as absurd as it is palpably untrue, if our experience, reason and observation are not greatly and mutually at fault. The leading Gentiles and anti-Mormon chiefs of Utah freely acknowledge that the legal assault upon polygamy is made with a view to breaking down the separate political autonomy of the Mormon people, but the Edmunds law has failed to accomplish anything in that direction; a few hundred polygamists, including some of the leaders of the Church, have been disfranchised, driven into exile, or compelled to remain in hiding, and many more have been sent to prison, but the entire Mormon populace has united in denouncing all this as the result of persecution, and in regarding the victims of the law as blessed martyrs, while the sufferings of innocent wives and blameless children have aroused the resentment and kindled the sympathy of every manly heart among them. Plural marriage complicates the Mormon question, but long before polygamy was announced as a doctrine of the Church, the Mormons were harassed and persecuted because of their unpopular faith and extreme religious devotion, quite as much as at present. The great

Mormon prophet, Joseph Smith, was murdered by a mob long before polygamy was known to the world as a tenet of Mormonism. There is no doubt in our mind but that polygamy, popularly practiced, as monogamy generally is, without the great restraints and solemn covenants of a profound religious faith, would tend to social demoralization, but the intensity and the peculiarity of the Mormon creed redeems plural marriage, practiced honestly, from its chief objectionable features, and, the Mormons claim, really exalts it into a marvel of social regeneration. It is sometimes maintained that polygamy violates the innate attributes of womanhood and extinquishes a cardinal feature of the female heart, but we find that the truth or falsity of this proposition depends wholly, or at least chiefly, upon education, training and the religious views and influences under which women live or are reared. Mormonism honestly and conscientiously espoused and faithfully adhered to modifies human nature itself; eradicates some native human sentiments and passions to a great extent, and develops new emotions and aspirations which are almost foreign to the balance of mankind. Extended, careful and close observation and enquiry among the Mormons will convince any intelligent and penetrating personal enquirer that this is true beyond question.

A great deal of popular prejudice in favor of enforced monogamy, and against the plural marriage system of the Mormons, is aroused by portraying beautiful and even ideal pictures of the American home and its

> "Two souls with but a single thought,
> Two hearts that beat as one,"

as contrasted with an altogether unfairly distorted plural household; and, as we understand the subject, neither the Mormon system nor the Mormon people would disparage, in the least, the happy, holy and complete union which is sometimes, but unfortunately not always, the result of the monogamous marriage. Certainly, far is it from the writer's heart to deprecate the home hallowed by the loving fusion of a true, chaste husband and one pure, devoted wife into the unity of perfect wedlock. Inviolable in its sanctity, pleasing in the sight of God and admirable in the estimation of all men, at all times, among the Mormons as well as among the Gentiles, must ever be a well-ordered, harmonious, monogamous domestic altar, around which one father and one mother gather their mutual offspring or live in peace and purity, ever tender and true to each other in all the varied family relationships, and, above all and over all, faithful and obedient to the Almighty's laws and every moral, social and physical amenity of life. The plural marriage of the Mormons does not profess to attack such a marital monogamous family condition to destroy it. Mormon polygamy only contemplates a remedy for faults and evils that have been coeval with monogamy; it does not ostensibly seek to undermine or vitiate the virtues, joys, glories or felicities of a properly ordained American home. If it did, we would execrate it with every drop of blood in our being; but while we admire and praise, and would protect even with our life, the principles which unite one man and one woman in graceful and blissful bonds, is there any reason why we should not at least equally respect and legally tolerate

> Three souls with but a single thought,
> Three hearts that beat as one?

The identity of offspring and insurmountable physical laws, as well as the fiat of God, render it immoral and wrong for a woman to have more than one husband at the same time, but if two women or more can love each other without jealousy or other flaw, and with each other's free consent, and even desire to be pure and true wives to the one true man, in the honest expectation of eternal exaltation, and a perpetuation of the plural relation in the transports of immortality beyond the veil, should the theoretical monogamist desire to interfere? And if so, why? We have heard much about the real and imaginary horrors of plural marriage—and no one will deny that plural households have been the occasional abodes of misery, just as monogamous households have been and are very frequently the scenes of revolting marital wretchedness and woe —but there are happy plural homes among the Mormons, or at least there were such in existence before the Edmunds law was put in force and many plural fathers consigned to prison or driven into exile. Let us take an impartial view of the brighter side of plurality as it has existed here in the Great Salt Lake basin. It is not fair to look only at the darker side in forming our opinion regarding the matter.

CHAPTER XXVII.

A Symposium of Personalities.—Conclusion.—Au Revoir.

IN anticipation of the publication of this book, the author has the pleasure of acknowledging the courtesies of several hundred subscribers who were willing to thus aid him to meet the expense of publication. Upon the list of these friends are the names of Mormons and Gentiles in about equal ratio to the respective local Mormon and Gentile population.

During the author's incarceration in Weber County Jail, which is located in the rear and basement of the Court House, at Ogden, he has to acknowledge the receipt of many courtesies at the hands of the County Court, County Clerk C. C. Richards, Sheriff Gilbert Belnap, H. H. Rolapp, Esq., and a multitude of country friends.

Through the regular and kind service of Mr. J. A. Lambert, whose especial care deserves especial mention, the prisoner was provided with excellent tonsorial facilities.

Mr. A. W. Millgate and Mr. E. H. Anderson, the incarcerated editor's former associates on the *Herald*, were ever ready to perform a kindly office for their less fortunate friend.

Mr. E. H. Anderson has long been the business manager of the *Herald*, and also Superintendent of Public Schools in Weber County, Utah. He is yet a young man, and procured all of his education in the Territory. He fills the duties of his public office ably and efficiently, and his personal character is that of a bright, pure and honest man. He is a Mormon from training and conviction.

It may not be wholly improper to note the author's impression of some of the cotemporaneously prominent men of Ogden, and Utah at large.

President John Taylor, the present chief leader of the Mormons, is a venerable man, nearly eighty years of age. It may be said that he is a graduate of the Mormon system. By virtue of his position at the head of the Church, his expressed will is more potent among the Mormons than that of any other authority in Utah. He is a wise but a poor man, and his management of the Church has been successful in a marked degree. Born in Westmorland County, England, November 1st, 1808, he secured a common school education, and became a local Methodist preacher. In 1832, he migrated from his native land to Canada. There he became noted as a great reform preacher, and was finally converted to Mormonism. Since then his whole life has been spent in the service of the Latter-day Church, with the history of which his name has been always prominently identified. He filled many important missions in Europe with the most gratifying success, and was wounded in Carthage Jail when the great Mormon prophet, Joseph Smith, was assassinated by a mob. When President Brigham Young died, John Taylor was president of the quorum of the Twelve Apostles. And as such he became the practical head of the Church, but it was not until 1880 that he was formally announced as "Prophet, Seer and Revelator," and as such the First President of the Church.

President John Taylor cannot fairly be compared with the illustrious late President, Brigham Young. While these two great First Presidents were richly endowed with many noble qualities in common, yet they must be considered essentially different in their greatness, because they both seem to have been especially prepared, and specifically qualified for leadership under different circumstances. President Brigham Young has been appropriately called the Moses of the Mormons. His talents eminently well qualified him for a leader upon such an occasion as the exodus of the Saints from the States, the settlement of Utah and the building of a broad foundation of a mighty colony. And President John Taylor seems to have been especially qualified to take up the great work where his stalwart, herculean predecessor left it.

Benign and just, bold, vigorous and courageous in character, President Taylor is personally a thoroughly accomplished man, full of profound earnestness, and overflowing with the genuine milk of human kindness. He has been not only a safe and sure guide, but also a true father to the Mormon people, who properly hold his name in the highest esteem and reverence and love.

Hon. George Q. Cannon, the first counselor, and nephew of President Taylor, and distinguished as the former Delegate to Congress from Utah, is the second in authority among the Mormons. He was born in Liverpool, England, January 11th, 1827, and came to this country with his parents when he was yet a small boy, and when the headquarters of the Saints was at Nauvoo. At an early day he was left an orphan, and later on he learned the printing business. In 1847, he came to Utah, and two years after proceeded to California, and thence to the Sandwich Islands, where he performed a most successful mission, introducing the Gospel among the natives, mastering the Kanaka tongue, and translating the Book of Mormon into that language. In 1854, he returned to Salt Lake Valley and performed a number of missions with success, and credit to himself. He established a paper in California, and then for awhile was editor of the *Deseret News*. Subsequently, he became private secretary to President Young, and, in the fall of 1872, he was elected Delegate to Congress, where he served the Territory with much ability and fidelity, until after the passage of the Edmunds law. In many respects he is a remarkable man —unusually adroit and perfectly urbane, scholarly, prudent, honest, and moreover thoroughly well acquainted with affairs of the world.

Hon. Joseph F. Smith, the second counselor to President Taylor, and a son of Hyrum Smith, the first Patriarch of the Church, is the third in authority among the Mormons. He was born at Far West, in Missouri, in 1838, about the time of the expulsion of the Mormons from that State by mob violence. He grew up amid the terribly stirring scenes that preceeded and followed the martyrdom of his father, and his uncle, the Prophet Joseph Smith. At the age of sixteen he filled a mission to the Sandwich Islands with gratifying success. Later he went to England in the service of the Church. In 1867, he became one of the Twelve Apostles, and since then he has served several times in the Legislature, and performed many important missions for the Church. He possesses an ardent sentient nature, is an eloquent speaker and writer.

President Taylor and his counselors, Cannon and Smith, are at present in retirement to avoid processes of the Federal courts, their alleged offenses being polygamous or unlawful cohabitation.

The next in authority among the Mormons are the Twelve Apostles. Albert Carrington, lately one of their number, was excommunicated not long ago, and the vacancy thus caused has not yet been filled.

Apostle Wilford Woodruff is the president of the Twelve. He is also Church Historian, and has the custody of the archives of the Church. He was born on the first of March, 1807, in the State of Connecticut, and is therefore over a year older than President Taylor. It was not until the year 1833 that he became a Mormon. Since then his life has been chiefly spent in mission work and in laying the granite foundation of the future of Utah. He springs from the grand old Puritan stock, and his whole life has been a noble exemplification of purity, fidelity and firm adherence to principle.

Apostle Franklin D. Richards was born in Massachusetts, April 2d, 1821. He also springs from illustrious Puritan stock. His boyhood was spent at hard manual labor, which he performed to aid his parents and secure himself much-coveted educational privileges. His frank, studious, enquiring, conscientious turn of mind prepared him early for the reception of the Latter-day Gospel, and he was baptized June 3d, 1838. That same year he left his native town for Far West, Missouri, where he arrived in due time. Shortly afterwards he entered the service of the Church and has filled many important missions with distinction and fidelity. He came to Salt Lake Valley in 1848, accompanied by his amiable and admirable wife, Mrs. Jane S. Richards, an excellent and devoted woman; and they together endured the pressing hardships which all the first settlers of the Territory were exposed to. On the twelfth of February, 1849, he was ordained an Apostle, and soon after he was summoned upon a mission to England, where he presided over the affairs of the Church, and won the most brilliant laurels in the performance of his holy calling. Subsequently, his life has been one continual series of splendid and laborious services for the Church, and for Utah. He has been several times elected a member of the Territorial Legislature, and his masterly mind and great experience gave him high rank as a legislator. Shortly after his return from a glorious European mission, in 1869, he was elected Probate Judge of Weber County, and in May of that year he took up his residence in Ogden, where he still resides. Ogden City was just then in need of the inspiring influences of a great and cultured mind, and the faithful, refined, and energetic Apostle Richards devoted himself with his accustomed zeal and success to the interests of the city, and the well-being of the people of Weber County. He founded a daily newspaper, advanced educational prospects, wrote, preached and labored personally to promote the diffusion of culture, refinement and moral worth. He was Probate Judge of Weber County continuously from 1869 until September, 1883, and proved beyond question the possession of the rarest judicial qualities. Overflowing with spontaneous goodness of heart, courteous, humane, generous, pure, scholarly and truly great and noble in all his attributes, the great Apostle, now nearly sixty-six years of age, is still in the prime of physical and intellectual vigor, a grand and gracious type of august manhood.

Apostle Lorenzo Snow, born April 3d, 1814, in Portage County, Ohio, is one of the most able, scholarly and accomplished of the living great Mormon leaders. In every respect he is a model disciple of the Savior. He is at present undergoing, in the Utah Penitentiary, an eighteen months' sentence for alleged unlawful cohabitation. Up to the time of his incarceration, from the early day when he first embraced the latter-day Gospel, his life has been passed in serving the Mormon Church and people with unflinching zeal and happy success. His deportment and moral attitude before the judge who sent him to prison were dignified and in heroic consonance with his life-long professions. His speech before the court when he was sentenced for the only offense which he was probably ever charged with, was typical of the modest and exalted spirit of the man and Apostle. Nothwithstanding his age, he bears his imprisonment patiently and well. As a missionary, a legislator, and a pioneer founder of Utah, his name will ever live in history, hallowed by the love and veneration of the whole Mormon people.

President D. H. Wells, born in Oneida County,

New York State, October 27th, 1814, is famous in the history of the Mormon Church, and his name has been prominently identified with the settlement and gradual progress of Utah, from the earliest times down to the present day. He became identified with the Mormons away back in the days when Nauvoo was in its primal prosperity. When Nauvoo fell, and the Mormon exodus began, he was the last to leave the doomed city. He came to Utah with the pioneers as aide-de-camp to President Brigham Young, and since then he has been second counselor to the First President of the Church, member of the Legislature, Superintendent of Public Works, Lieutenant-General of the Utah militia, Mayor of Salt Lake City for several terms, and in the meanwhile he has performed several foreign missions. President Wells springs from an illustrious and patriotic American ancestry, and his life has been fruitful, successful and eventful, indeed. He and Hon. John W. Young are counselors to the Twelve.

Apostle Francis M. Lyman, was born in the State of Illinois, January 12th, 1840. He is a son of the distinguished late Mormon Apostle Amasa Lyman, who was a second cousin of Henry Ward Beecher and the noted Harriet

Beecher Stowe. The present Apostle is a man of large caliber and great intellectual ability. He has served the Church with remarkable fidelity for many years in many different capacities, and has especially distinguished himself as the presiding officer of the lower branch of the Utah Legislature. His forefathers and kinsmen, for several generations back, have been foremost in the ranks of American patriots and figured both as civil and military heroes in the most momentous past history of this continent. Education, experience and the mental greatness which he has happily inherited, all combine with the noblest graces of manhood in the person of Apostle Lyman.

Apostle John Henry Smith was born at Winter Quarters, near Council Bluffs, Iowa, September 18, 1848. He is a son of the former Apostle and pioneer, George A. Smith. The present Apostle Smith spent the early part of his youth working upon his mother's farm at Provo. In 1874, he filled a mission to Europe. The next year he was ordained Bishop of the Seventeenth Ward, in Salt Lake City, and in 1880 he was elevated to the Apostleship. He was cashier of the Utah Central Railway for a number of years. Every position that he occupied was filled with honor to himself and satisfaction to the people. He is popular, manly and kind-hearted, as well as prudent and sagacious.

Apostle Erastus Snow was one of the first Mormon settlers of Utah. He was born in the State of Vermont, November 9th, 1818. His family settled in Massachusetts in colonial days, and were typical Americans of those heroic times. The Apostle became a Mormon in 1833, and in the same year began to preach the Gospel. In September, 1847, he became one of the Twelve Apostles. He subsequently established and fostered a great and successful branch mission of the Church in Scandinavia, filled numerous missions with honor and fidelity, served repeatedly in the Territorial Legislature with distinction as the representative of southern Utah—a section of the country which owes its successful settlement and general development largely to his genius.

Apostle John W. Taylor is a distinguished son of the President of the Church. Among the younger Apostles he is a bright and glowing light. He inherits much of his illustrious father's quiet firmness and indomitable courage and devotion. He is a pure man, who believes in all that he teaches, and as a consequence of his aggressive energy in defending the Church he has recently been made the object of judicial action in Idaho, where he is still under indictment for the alleged incitement of rebellion against the laws of the United States.

Apostle Brigham Young, Jr., is an illustrious son of the celebrated great First President of the Mormon Church, whose name he bears. He is a staunch and brilliant supporter of the Gospel and the cause of the Church, towards the prestige of which his father contributed so much.

Apostle Moses Thatcher, one of the most eloquent and scholarly of men, and withal a profound thinker, occupies an exalted and responsible position in the Apostolic quorum. He is a man of proverbially pure and honest character, and any cause would find a powerful support in his adherence and devotion.

Apostle Heber J. Grant, one of the younger members of the quorum of the Twelve, springs from a famous and hardy ancestry, to which he is destined to lend additional lustre. He is credited with remarkably brilliant business and financial talents, and is in every respect a thorough gentleman, honest of heart, dignified in deportment, stately in personal bearing, courteous and upright.

Apostle George Teasdale, with whose record we

are unacquainted, completes the list of the present Apostles of the Mormon Church. Upon them, in a great measure, must depend the nobler destinies of Utah and the issue of the present irrepressible conflict between Saint and Gentile in this powerful and rich Territory. There are many other influential and able men among the Mormons—such as William B. Preston, the Presiding Bishop of the whole Church, a manly and admirable soul—who are elevated to power among the Mormons, but it would require whole volumes to enumerate them all properly.

The subordinate authorities in the Mormon Church may be described as regimental army officers, while President John Taylor may be likened to a commander-in-chief, with his counselors, Cannon and Smith, as aids, and the quorum of the Twelve Apostles as staff officers.

These dignitaries, immediately or through their subordinates in the Priesthood, nominate all parties for ecclesiastical office, and the Priesthood, over which these stand in chief authority, usually, though not always, pre-arrange nominations to civil office, formally and openly made through the People's Party in Utah. The masses are given the privilege of endorsing or rejecting all nominees, both civil and ecclesiastical which are thus made—a right often used with much liberty, especially with the nominations for civil offices.

Presidents of Stakes in the Mormon system may be likened unto colonels of regiments in an army. Their ecclesiastical jurisdiction is usually co-extensive with the boundaries of a county, and each one often holds a county office also. A Stake President gets no salary, as such, but of course, when a civil officer, has the emoluments attached to any civil office which he may hold.

Hon. A. O. Smoot, President of Utah Stake, and residing in Utah County, is an astute, careful business man of much general experience. His judgment on all subjects is always eminently practical and generally sound. He has been long in the Church, and is now venerable with age. He is typical of the class of men usually chosen for rulers among the Mormons; above all things, he professes to be devoted to the Church of which he has long been a staunch and stalwart pillar.

Hon. Abram Hatch, President of Wasatch Stake, is a somewhat younger man than President Smoot, but like the latter, Mr. Hatch is rich, prudent and practical.

Hon. Angus M. Cannon, the President of Salt Lake Stake, which embraces Salt Lake City, and County, is a brother of Hon. George Q.

Cannon, of the First Presidency of the Church. He is likewise prudent and practical, and distinguished for long and faithful service under the heads of the Church. The same may be said of Presidents C. O. Card, of Cache Stake, O. G. Snow, of Box Elder Stake, and most of the balance of Stake Presidents, who number thirty in all.

Hon. Caleb W. West, formerly of Kentucky, is the present Governor of Utah Territory. His Excellency was appointed by President Cleveland, and has thus far given all classes of the people a fair degree of satisfaction. He is in the prime of life, and has had a considerable judicial experience. He is evidently a man of brains, and endowed also with great firmness and courage. He favors the enforcement of the Edmunds law, and may be regarded as the leader, *ex officio*, of those who are determined to promote what the non-Mormons of Utah are pleased to consider as proper Federal supremacy over the Territory. Governor West is a Democrat, and his personal character is noble and admirable.

Hon. John T. Caine, Delegate to Congress from Utah, was born January 8th, 1829, near the town of Peel, Isle of Man. He became a Mormon in 1847, and afterwards came to Utah, and performed many missions for the Church. He has served several terms in the Utah Legislature, and is widely known in Utah as a journalist. He held the office of Recorder in Salt Lake City when he was first elected as Delegate to Congress, in 1876. During the last two years, as a Delegate, he has done immense service for the Territory and the people who elected him, by protecting their interests intelligently and well at Washington.

Hon. Arthur L. Thomas, the present Territorial Secretary, is a Republican. He has held his office for some time, and is endowed with a happy faculty of avoiding offensive partisanship in a community where such a course is next to impossible. He is a compact, energetic, dexterous and amiable, polished little man, and, without doubt, an efficient officer. Recently he has been appointed a member of the Utah Commission.

The present United States Marshal of Utah is Mr. Frank H. Dyer. He has held the office only a few months, but has done his utmost to arrest the largest possible number of alleged offenders under the Edmunds law. He was formerly engaged in the mines at Park City, Utah, and has a high reputation for personal integrity and business ability. Mr. H. E. Steele is Mr. Dyer's deputy in Ogden.

Hon. C. S. Zane is the Chief Justice of Utah. He is a Republican, and has occupied the supreme bench of the Territory for over two years. During that time His Honor has made himself somewhat odious, locally, by the manner in which his court has enforced the Edmunds law; but upon all matters, not touching the Mormon question, he is universally conceded to be a scholarly lawyer and an honest judge, who renders his judicial decisions according to the best of his knowledge and ability. His Honor's errors—and he has doubtless committed some, for he is human—*et humanum est errare* – have been those of the head rather than those of the heart or conscience. This the author states with the greater pleasure because he has been falsely accused of libeling the Chief Justice deliberately and with actual personal malice.

The present Associate Justices of the Utah Supreme Court are Hon. Jacob S. Boreman and Hon. H. P. Henderson. The former is a Republican, and has occupied the bench for some time. Judge Henderson is a Democrat, but recently appointed an Associate Justice by President Cleveland. He enjoys a high reputation as a thorough gentleman and able legal scholar, and thus far His Honor has made a very fair and creditable judicial record.

Hon. W. H. Dickson, the United States District Attorney for Utah, is a Republican. He has held the office for a number of years, and won a considerable reputation for personal and professional persistency. As a lawyer he is undoubtedly keen, determined and subtle. He has been regarded as the chief anti-Mormon of the Territory, and his friends are never tired of extolling his name. His present assistants are C. S. Varian, Ogden Hiles and Colonel Vic Bierbower. The last named prosecuted Apostle Lorenzo Snow to conviction and consequent imprisonment. Messrs. Varian and Hiles are good subordinates.

The present editors of the Salt Lake City daily papers are all notable men. Charles W. Penrose, the editor-in-chief of the *Deseret Evening News*, the official organ of the Mormon Church, is now in exile to avoid prosecution under the Edmunds law, but still contributes to the editorial columns of the paper. He is undoubtedly the greatest of all the present professional journalists of Utah. As a poet he is justly celebrated among the Mormons, who owe to his lyric genius many noble anthems that never fail to arouse the enthusiasm and zeal of the Latter-day Saints whenever they are sang. He is a sentient, eloquent, impressive, logical and convincing editorial writer, and justly celebrated for his unflagging energy and activity.

Judge C. C. Goodwin, the chief editor of the Salt Lake anti-Mormon organ, is also a brilliant writer and a poet. He possesses some literary talents of a high order, but often uses them in a manner that excites the pity and contempt of those who would otherwise be his admirers.

Byron Groo, a native of Utah, is the polished and distinguished editor of the Salt Lake *Herald*, the leading independent paper of the Territory. Mr. Groo is a bright ornament of the journalistic profession, and an urbane, accomplished gentleman.

Among the business men of Salt Lake City, Walker Brothers, Henry Dinwoodey, H. S. Eldredge and John Sharp are eminently representative of the pioneer enterprise and sagacity which have given Utah a place in the first rank of financiers. Walker Brothers are non-Mormons; Messrs. Dinwoodey, Eldredge and Sharp are Mormons. All have large fortunes which they have accumulated in Utah.

Ogden City, the second place in size and importance in Utah, contains about as many non-

Mormon residents as Latter-day Saints. It is here that the writer is chiefly acquainted personally. Among the individual merchants of the place, Fred. J. Kiesel, Esq., of the wholesale grocery house of the Kiesel Co., is a non-Mormon of great business ability and enterprise, as is amply proven by the abundance of his success. He is of German origin—a large-souled man of liberal, tolerant, progressive views and generous sentiments.

Mr. John Watson, the genial manager of the Ogden branch Z. C. M. I., is a young but an exceedingly able, enterprising and prudent business man.

Hon. D. H. Peery, the present Mayor of Ogden, is an eminently adroit capitalist. As a financier, he has few peers in Utah, or, indeed, anywhere else in the world. He is a Mormon of advanced views, and was formerly repeatedly a member of the Utah Legislature, and for a time President of Weber Stake.

Hon. L. W. Shurtliff, President of Weber Stake, and Probate Judge of Weber County, was a member of the last Utah Legislature. Before he became Stake President he was unknown as a public officer, but had been Bishop of Plain City.

Among the most adroit, persevering and able energetic and successful business men of Ogden,

Sidney Stevens, Esq., takes high and honorable rank. He is one of those firm, independent, self-sustaining and manly gentlemen who always leave golden footprints on the sands of time.

Hon. Lorin Farr has the honor of being the founder of Ogden and the first Mayor of the city. He was also the first President of Weber Stake, and has served repeatedly in the Utah Legislature. He was born in Vermont, July 27th, 1820, and he springs from genuine Puritan ancestors. He joined the Church in 1832, and has been prominently identified with it ever since. As a missionary, a thrifty pioneer, and the father of a large and interesting family, his career has been alike honorable and useful. He has been prominently identified with the material development of Weber County from the first, and established the woolen mills in Ogden, where he also owns and conducts a flour mill.

A. Kuhn & Brother, an old general merchandise wholesale and retail house, deserves to be placed in the first rank of the successful business establishments of Ogden. The two brothers, who conduct the destinies of their house on principles that never fail of success, are extremely politic, reliable and prudent, as is evinced by their success, which has enabled them to build and stock one of the very largest and finest three story brick business blocks in Ogden.

Bishop E. Stratford, of the Fourth Ward, in Ogden, and his son, Jesse, are excellent specimens of the stubborn commercial ability which has become famous, in its development, under the aegis of the Mormon system. They are the proprietary of the great wholesale and retail furniture house of E. Stratford & Son.

Mr. H. M. Bond, the active Ogden commission merchant and grocer, is a gentleman of first-class business and noble personal qualifications. Such men as he would make efficient supports to the commerce of the most enterprising cities in the world.

Judge P. H. Emerson, a leading citizen of Ogden, and one of the brightest and noblest ornaments of the Utah bar, was for twelve years Associate Justice of the Supreme Court of the Territory. By nature large-souled, hospitable, generous and social, the Judge is a deservedly popular man. His legal talents, too, are of the highest order; his learning extensive and profound, and his eloquence polished and effective, alike in pathos, invective and argument.

Hon. Franklin S. Richards, a son of the eminent Apostle, F. D. Richards, is in some respects the most remarkable man in Utah. He is the possessor of a peculiarly brilliant mind, which qualifies him for the most illustrious paths of life. Although, as yet, comparatively a young man, he has become celebrated as the great Mormon constitutional lawyer. His intellect is symmetrical, well-balanced, expansive and comprehensive; his genius altogether of a high quality, which predestines him to the grandest stations of honor and power, if he lives. Although his residence is now in Salt Lake City, Ogden still claims a share of the honor, as having been his former home.

Mr. Lamoni Grix, a quiet business man, who rarely intrudes himself in an ostentatious way upon the public, is yet a generous, public-spirited and enterprising tradesman.

Mr. A. G. Harris, the leading Ogden greengrocer, has won a deserved marked success, by non-partisan conservativeness, that has been alike honorable and prudent.

Mr. L. B. Adams is an eminent factor in the business community of the junction city. He is a conservative non-Mormon, and, withal, a popular, prudent man.

Mr. C. L. Peebles, a non-Mormon druggist, of Ogden, has built up a flourishing extensive business, and personally he is an agreeable and polished gentleman who will bear acquaintance.

Mr. J. S. Lewis was at one time the Liberal candidate for Mayor of Ogden. He is a successful, rich, magnanimous, conservative and generous business man, and his capacious head contains many stronger and deeper views than he is in the habit of expressing.

Mr. William Driver, the generous and wholesouled proprietor of the "City Drug Store," and member of the City Council, is endowed with much natural ability, and he occupies an important position in local business and official circles.

Among the younger, enterprising, successful and shrewd general merchandise dealers of the west, Mr. James Wotherspoon has established a solid and thriving business by the exercise of the foremost commercial qualities.

Mr. J. A. Stephens, the Ogden merchandise broker, has been long and favorably known throughout this inter-mountain region, and his new and commodious quarters on Main Street are a fitting testimonial of his eminent success.

The newly-appointed postmaster of Ogden, Mr. John Tyler, is an estimable gentleman, long and always favorably known in this community as clerk of the Broom Hotel. He is admirably qualified to succeed the efficient and well-liked retiring postmaster, Major E. A. Littlefield.

Messrs. Rubel & Penglase have rapidly and thoroughly founded a large and profitable wholesale liquor trade, and occupy large sales and store rooms in the elegant and extensive new building of A. Kuhn & Bro.

The mammoth roller flour mills of Messrs. Peery & Mack are the finest and largest in this section of the world—something that Ogden is justly proud of, and another of the many local enterprises largely creditable to the thrift and sagacity of Hon. D. H. Peery.

A. R. Haywood, Esq., although, as yet, but a young member of the Ogden bar, is a thorough gentleman of integrity and capacity, which will yet lead him to a place among the most successful disciples of Blackstone.

The registration officer of Ogden, Mr. B. L. Stephens, is a venerable gentleman and a veteran soldier of the Union. He has made a very satisfactory registrar.

Mr. Thomas Cahoon, the Ogden coal merchant, is a deservedly popular gentleman. He has built up an extensive and profitable business and merited success by enterprise and fair dealing.

Mr. Nath. Kuhn, the well-known wholesale

Ogden cigar merchant, has every qualification to ensure thrift in business, as his continued liberal success attests.

Mr. David Eccles, the Ogden lumber merchant, is a self-made man, whose ample means have been accumulated through the exercise of the most modest and yet brilliant business ability. He has recently purchased a great lumber business in Oregon.

Mr. S. M. Preshaw is a noteworthy Ogden character. He is a first-rate undertaker, contractor and builder, and might have been a very successful philosopher.

Mr. W. H. Wright, of the firm of Wright & Sons, deserves a prominent place in the galaxy of the celebrated business men of Ogden. From the basis of a small capital he has speedily built up a flourishing establishment, which to-day ranks among the foremost in Ogden.

Equally distinguished as a fine prose writer, poet and physician is Dr. A. S. Condon, of the junction city.

Dr. J. X. Allen, the eminent physician and surgeon, has a host of friends among the people here.

The genial H. A. Clawson, of the Depot Hotel, in Ogden, is unrivalled as a caterer, and his tables are ever laden with good things as his heart is filled with genial sentiments.

Mr. W. J. Wood has introduced a popular novelty in this business community, which is a variety shop, appropriately called the "Plunder Store."

Peerless among the tobacco and cigar manufacturers of the west is Mr. C. B. Payson, of Ogden, who is also personally one of the most sensible and enterprising of gentlemen.

Mr. George A. Lowe may be classed among the shrewdest and, withal, the most enterprising of Ogden business men, among whom he may be ranked, because of his large emporium of farm machinery, wagons and the like, in the junction city, although he really resides in Salt Lake City, where are also the headquarters of the Co-operative Wagon and Machine Co., which has a large branch establishment in Ogden, and with which Apostle H. J. Grant, and others eminent among the Mormons, are identified. Mr. Sidney Stevens, of Ogden, also deals in wagons, farm machinery, mill machinery, wagons, etc., and his headquarters are in Ogden, where he lives. These three concerns represent great business talent and large capital.

There are few men in Ogden or elsewhere,

either in business or following a profession, who are more deservedly popular than the sensible, just, liberal and good-natured veteran, Colonel J. E. Hudson.

Mr. Jesse J. Driver, the amiable and careful druggist, is an enterprising, thorough gentleman of no ordinary calibre. Ogden already recognizes him as one of her most successful and beneficent business men.

Among the strongest types of conscientious Mormon pioneers of Utah, the venerable Mr. Richard Ballantyne deserves exceeding high rank. His large and interesting family of highly respectable, staunch sons and daughters, are a credit to Utah. And his whole life has been one of supreme devotion to the cause of God and humanity, as he has honestly conceived his duty to be with a belief no less than sublime.

C. C. Richards, Esq., an able son of Apostle F. D. Richards, and the Prosecuting Attorney of Weber County, is a young lawyer whose future is destined to add lustre to the annals of the Utah bar.

Percival J. Barrett, Esq., has an enviable reputation as a lawyer, which is only eclipsed by his reputation as a discreet and pleasant, cultured gentleman, while his amiable and attractive wife rivals even her excellent husband in the way of social hospitality.

Judge R. K. Williams, formerly Chief Justice of Kentucky, has perhaps passed the best days of a long and illustrious career, and he will leave behind the impress of his lofty character on the great future of Ogden City.

Associated with the Judge in the legal business at present is the late distinguished United States Prosecuting Attorney of Idaho, Hon. W. R. White, who proposes to locate permanently in the junction city, where he has as yet resided only a brief time.

Though somewhat difficult of approach and eccentric, in our experience, Captain Ransford Smith, formerly Liberal candidate for Delegate to Congress from Utah, is reputed to be a most urbane gentleman, with a kind heart, as well as he is known to be a persistent and scholarly attorney-at-law.

It is fortunate for the industry of manufacturing boots and shoes in Ogden that the business is supported in part by two such thorough business men as Mr. Thomas Ashby and Mr. Joshua Small. They occupy a somewhat similar position in the boot and shoe manufacturing trade as Mr. W. S. Read and Mr. G. W. Snively occupy in the business of manufacturing harness and saddles, or that Mr. T. W. Jones, the prince of local merchant tailors, occupies in the merchant tailoring trade. Each of these gentlemen are expert in their line and Mr. Jones is especially endowed with that genius of progress and enterprise which gives a city life and wealth.

Among the Ogden veterans whose courage and patriotism entitle them to the first consideration, is General Nathan Kimball. His record as a soldier, during the war of the Rebellion, will go down to remotest generations for admiration and imitation. The General's son, J. N. Kimball, Esq., is one of the most subtle, keen and adroit of Ogden lawyers.

In some respects Mr. E. J. Wagner, of the wholesale and retail clothing establishment of E. J. Wagner & Co., is a wondrously sound business philosopher. He is intent upon building up a sound and permanent business, and his methods are as remarkably just, deep and clear as his views are enterprising and progressive, all of which is emphatically proven by the magnitude of his trade in Ogden and elsewhere.

Among the more retiring lawyers, and yet most estimable gentlemen to be met anywhere, A. H. Nelson, Esq., is respected by all who know him.

Among the younger and more enterprising, and therefore successful grocery and produce dealers, Mr. F. D. Higginbotham has already won a substantial place, which unmistakably foretells his future thrift.

Mr. A. Hindenlang, though he made an unostentatious beginning, is rapidly advancing in the scale of merited prosperity as a jeweler and watchmaker, where he will speedily take a front rank.

Messrs. Hopkins & Co. and Corey Brothers are flourishing and first-class non-Mormon grocers, who have fortified themselves in business extensively and considerately.

Ogden is particularly fortunate in the possession of three reliable and well-conducted banking institutions. The Utah National Bank is ably and securely officered by Mr. J. E. Dooley, president; Mr. W. N. Shilling, vice-president; and Mr. L. B. Adams, cashier. Mr. Dooley is not only an expert financier, but also an able, sagacious, prudent and conservative, liberal-minded gentleman. Mr. Shilling is not less happily qualified to command respect and esteem, as are all of those officially connected with this enterprising, solid concern.

Mr. H. C. Harkness is president and Mr. O.

E. Hill is cashier of that excellent, reliable repository and exchange medium widely known as the Commercial National Bank of Ogden. With these two efficient officers and admirable gentlemen, such solid capitalists and astute, progressive financiers as David Eccles, J. S. Lewis, M. Buchmiller, J. C. Armstrong, Adam Patterson and Henry Conant are associated as directors.

The First National Bank of Ogden City enjoys the distinction of having, for cashier, a stalwart son of Brigham Young, the late great Mormon leader. The business affairs of this prosperous concern are conducted with extreme caution and unfailing prudence, as indeed would be patent from the fact that Hon. D. H. Peery is prominently connected with its management.

Mr. Barnard White, an old, esteemed and substantial resident of Ogden, is the quiet possessor of a happily constituted nature, which has eminently well qualified him for success in business and prominence in society. He is a member of the extensive, general merchandise establishment of Burton, Herrick & White, and sole proprietor of a great lumber business in the junction city.

The versatile and physically rather diminutive Mr. B. F. Hurlbut, the druggist, has a genial soul as much larger and a business enterprise as much greater as his physical proportions are less imposing than many other men.

Mr. Ambrose Greenwell, Sr., though an inmate of the Utah Penitentiary for conscience' sake, at present, has perhaps more friends among all classes of people in Ogden than any other man. He is the veteran meat market proprietor of the city, and as rich, substantial and genial as he is popular.

Mr. Mark Lindsey, the veteran Fifth Street vendor of ice cream, confectionery, cigars and the like, is a man of strong character and generous impulses.

Among the rising young attorneys of Ogden, Nathan Tanner, Jr., is worthy of especial consideration.

Far and wide throughout this section of Utah Mr. Ben. E. Rich, at present Recorder for Weber County, is known and admired as a versatile and enterprising genius.

The mammoth wholesale and retail furniture and carpet establishment of Boyle & Co. is noted in Ogden, and indeed throughout the entire Territory, for enterprise, fair dealing and success, and to Mr. John A. Boyle is due a great portion of the firm's prosperity. Although comparatively a young man, he has won golden laurels as an astute business man, a musician and a municipal legislator. Genial, generous and accommodating, his popularity is only equaled by his genuine goodness of heart.

Mr. Warren G. Child, Sr., of the well-known general merchandise firm of Child & Son, is one of the staunch early settlers of this inter-mountain region, now well advanced in the shade of many honorable years. He is a solid and capable business man, generous and firm in friendship, and the head of a large and thrifty flourishing family that honors the paternal name.

There are in the West few if any more quiet and yet persevering and sound business men than Browning Brothers, the Ogden gunsmiths and wholesale and retail dealers in guns, ammunition and sporting goods.

Mr. W. H. Stevens is an affable and enterprising gentleman, and his large business in the line of arms, ammunition and sporting goods is constantly increasing.

Roy & Company, a comparatively new commission merchant house of Ogden, already manifest a vim and enterprise that must attain success if continued.

Messrs. Keck & Tavey, proprietors of a leading general merchandise house in Ogden, are both pleasant and reliable gentlemen to do business with, and personally progressive and generous.

Messrs. Snyder & Burt are equally prepossessing merchants, and their large dry goods establishment is a model of elegance.

Mr. George H. Tribe is a most estimable and considerate capitalist, and his handsome and large general merchandise and carpet emporium is a feature of the junction city.

Messrs. Clark & Shaw are personally courteous, liberal, substantial and enterprising gentlemen, and their extensive general merchandise house commands a justly large patronage.

Messrs. D. H. Peery & Sons' general merchandise establishment occupies a leading position in the business arena of Ogden. At the head of this firm is the great Utah financier, Hon. D. H. Peery, Sr., and among the sons associated with him D. H. Peery, Jr., promises to even rival his distinguished father as a sound business man.

Messrs. Burton, Herrick & White transact a large annual business in the general merchandise and hardware line, and the proprietors are three of the most sagacious and prominent old residents of Ogden.

Among the prudent and substantial leading

men of Ogden, Mr. Samuel Horrocks has long been favorably known. His able son is associated with him in the general merchandise business.

Mr. W. W. Funge, proprietor of the extensive wholesale and retail hardware and tinware house, is a determined and enterprising business man, who is personally frank, social and generous.

Messrs. John Scowcroft & Son, manufacturers of confectionery and dealers in general merchandise, have built up a large and profitable business by fair dealing and enterprise.

Mr. John Smuin and Mr. Thomas G. Thomas, of the wholesale and retail general merchandise house of Smuin & Thomas, occupy a foremost place among the prosperous business men of the city. Personally they are both, deservedly, favorites of the public.

The commission merchants of Ogden have a public-spirited and successful representative in the person of Mr. H. L. Griffin. By assiduous exertion and business tact of the first order, he has built up a splendid shipping business, and personally he is one of those decisive, indomitable characters who succeed in all they undertake.

Mr. James Thompson, manufacturer of tinware and dealer in hardware, is an energetic and firm gentleman and his business is sure to prosper with the progress of Ogden.

Mr. Robert P. Harris and his brother Winfield S. Harris, have built up a large and profitable business as dealers in fruit and produce, under the •firm name of Harris Brothers. They are courteous and reliable gentlemen.

Mr. H. C. Wardleigh, the proprietor of the Ogden Music Temple, is a veteran soldier of the Union, and an enterprising, high-minded, patriotic business man of ability and energy.

Mr. Willard Kay, the senior member of the late flourishing and active house of W. Kay & Co., produce dealers and commission merchants, is one of Utah's most sagacious, thrifty and admirable sons, and his brother, associated with him in business, is no less affable, prudent and reliable.

Among the newer business establishments of Ogden, the house of Messrs. Eldredge, Pratt & Company, dealers in musical instruments and sewing machines, has already won an extensive patronage and general confidence.

Mr. Isadore Marks, the member of the great leading wholesale and retail clothing establishment of Marks, Goldsmith & Company, is a remarkably cautious, astute and enterprising business man. His house has won an enviable reputation and a fair patronage through the wisdom and prudence of Mr. Marks.

Mr. J. M. Russell and E. M. Marcus have laid upon a solid foundation a prosperous business in the line of leather, hides and wool. They are personally most agreeable gentlemen to deal with.

Mr. P. A. Herdti, the Fifth Street grocer, is a brisk, bright and popular gentleman, whose business is yet destined to assume the most splendid proportions.

Personally Dr. H. J. Powers is one of the most urbane and accommodating of men, and professionally, as a physician and surgeon, he has established a reputation in Ogden that is singularly perfect and happy.

Dr. John D. Carnahan is another favorite and thoroughly accomplished physician and surgeon, who has won golden opinions in Ogden both professionally and personally.

Mr. D. D. Jones, of the Idaho Lumber Company, which does a fine business, is not only a first-class architect and builder, but a gentleman of many admirable personal qualities, and a profound student of the business conditions of this Territory, and of the commercial capabilities of Ogden.

There are few men in business in Ogden, or indeed elsewhere, who have more sterling business qualifications or more amiable and congenial personal attributes than Mr. Theo. Schaunsenbach, the secretary and treasurer of the F. J. Kiesel Co.

Recently the new drug firm of Cunningham & Co. have promisingly entered the business arena in Ogden. Mr. Frank Cunningham, who manages the establishment, is a thorough chemist and a popular young gentleman.

The writer regrets that the space at his disposal forbids even the further enumeration of the business men of Ogden. And he regrets, also, that, for the same reason, he has been compelled to be so brief in this reference to many of the gentlemen who worthily represent the great commercial interests of this thriving and prosperous municipality. However, Mr. Hemenway contents himself at present with the proposal to write a full and accurate history of the pioneers, merchants and manufacturers of the junction city, and in that work he hopes to more fully set forth his high estimation and cordial appreciation not only of the gentlemen whom he has so briefly mentioned, but of others whom space will not permit him to represent here.

With a firm and profound belief in the future great commercial destiny of Ogden, and after having experienced the unbounded kindness and liberality of the good citizens of this city, the author rejoices that the erection of a grand Union Depot in this city will give new and final confidence in the permanent importance of the place as a commercial and railway centre. And in this connection he ventures to suggest that the junction city ought to have a representative newspaper—a paper which all business men could unite in sustaining and which would thus command the confidence of the people. The writer feels confident that such a journal is possible—a commercial and household journal removed alike from vicious partisanship on the one hand and gagged mincing neutrality on the other hand. Party spirit is often so fierce and intolerant in this country that common commercial, manufacturing and agricultural interests are divided and arrayed against each other by a radical journalistic partisanship which is in reality beneficial to nobody. Of course the editor of a milk and water non-partisan sheet would be restrained from saying what his conscience proclaimed on the most vital commercial and agricultural topics, and this is not the sort of a paper that could live long anywhere. But between the extremes of rabid partisanship on the one hand and gagged neutrality on the other, the writer believes there is a happy medium—a position from which a journal may openly and heartily advocate the principles and commend the measures of that party to which its connections ally it, yet frankly dissent from its party's course on a particular question, and even denounce its party candidates if they were shown to be deficient in capacity, or, far worse, in integrity. A journal thus loyal to its guiding convictions, yet ready to expose or condemn unworthy conduct or incidental error on the part of the men attached to its party, must be far more effective, even party-wise, than though it may always be counted on to applaud or reprobate, bless or curse, as the party's prejudices or immediate interests might seem to prescribe. Such a journal, devoted primarily, first, last, midst and at all times to the commercial, manufacturing and agricultural interests of Ogden and vicinity, and further devoted to the dissemination of pure and reliable news, would not only be a great friend to the business men of Ogden but a blessing to the people of the entire Territory. Such a paper, we venture to hope, will yet be established by the business men of Ogden.

Since this book was mostly written the author, Charles W. Hemenway, has been released from jail and restored to liberty through the kindness of Chief Justice C. S. Zane, and the executive clemency of His Excellency, Governor Caleb W. West. He entered upon the term of his imprisonment in Weber County Jail, July 29th, 1886, and was pardoned on the fifteenth of November following. He thus escaped eight and a half months of his original sentence, and besides cherishing lively sensations of gratitude towards the Governor who granted, and the Chief Justice who recommended, his pardon, he is happy to address the reader his choicest benedictions while once again breathing the air of freedom. *Au Revoir.*

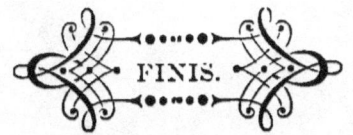

APPENDIX A.

AN OPEN TESTAMENTARY LETTER.

To His Excellency Governor Caleb W. West, His Honor Chief Justice Charles S. Zane, the non-Mormons of Ogden and the People of the United States:

FELLOW CITIZENS:—As the first breath which I inhaled in infancy was drawn from the atmosphere of American freedom, and the first lessons instilled into my youthful heart by parental care taught me to believe that American liberty was a grand and glorious guarantee of individual equality and impartial justice to all men under the sovereignty of the greatest republic on earth; and, whereas, from the earliest years of my understanding, I have gratefully thanked heaven that I was born in "the land of the free and the home of the brave," and with a steadfast faith continually have ever looked in most implicit confidence to the sovereign people for redress from public wrongs, for protection in the pursuit of happiness, for sympathy in misfortune, and, above all, for defense from the hideous monsters of persecution and oppression, therefore do I now appeal to the chief executive and judicial authority of the American Territory in which I now live, and to the people of the whole country as well—not that I have any private grievance which alone entitles me to a hearing before such an august tribunal, but rather because that in connection with the public treatment of my humble self, as a native-born, true and loyal American citizen, I have witnessed, here in Utah, a great and lamentable perversion of public justice, which in principle and effect at least—if not in enormity—equals the most dangerous and repulsive aspects of monarchial favoritism and Asiatic tyranny.

As I live and love the mother who gave me birth and reared me through infancy with maternal loving kindness and tender, prayerful care; as I hope for immortality beyond the clouds of death, and pray that the last time my eyes shall be permitted to behold the light of day, it may illumine an undivided and sanctified Union, a free and happy people preserved in peace and unity by justice administered with equality, and exalted by the universal abolition of persecution or tyrannical discriminations under the stars and stripes; as I live, so do I, without malice or the remotest desire for revenge, state truly all the essential facts in the following case, which I beg you will candidly consider and adjudicate in your own hearts, at least.

In the first months of the year 1884, a young stranger, then in the twenty-fourth year of his age, came to Utah. He was an American, and had acquired some proficiency in the profession of a newspaper writer. He had spent the whole of his few adult years in a studious, sober, honest pilgrimage through distant lands, that he might, by observation and experience, gather wisdom withal. In traveling as a stranger from place to place he had always and everywhere sought out the purest and best people with whom to associate himself, and when circumstances prevented him from forming social relationships with the better class in any community, he contented himself by remaining aloof and alone. Following this invariable rule of his, when he came to Utah, he affiliated with some humble, somewhat unpolished, but pure and honest people who happened to profess a religion called Mormonism. In the course of time he expressed his opinions in favor of these peculiar religionists, but without, at that time at least, abusing their enemies, when forthwith the Salt Lake *Tribune* began to abuse him scurrilously and personally. A few months later he accepted a position as editor of a Mormon newspaper, and removed to Ogden. A few few months later still, he was unfortunate enough to publish three several articles, which were founded upon reports that reached him from various apparently reliable sources, and his first intimation that these articles were considered libels came in the form of assault, arrest and indictment. As he was a total stranger to the parties considered libeled, it was manifest that he could have had no personal malice in the premises; nevertheless, without being given an opportunity to correct any errors he may have inadvertently made, he was forced to trial before a jury composed exclusively of his political enemies, without being able to secure any legal protection, and, as a matter of course, convicted in one case; and foreseeing like inevitable consequences in the two remaining cases pending against him, he pleaded guilty in each instance as a mere formality to save trouble and time. The Court, of its own motion, suspended sentence, in part, for a time, but eventually taxed him large sums repeatedly, and consigned him to jail for one year for one alleged libel upon a person who did not know of the existence of the alleged libelous article until after the accused was indicted by an exclusively hostile partisan grand jury. In the case tried, where the party chiefly aggrieved, as a prosecuting witness, upon oath swore that the alleged libel upon him did him no harm, but perhaps did him some good, the accused stranger editor was taxed $200 and costs, $85. He was too poor to meet this sum, and a generous public came to his relief in that instance, but the subsequent penalties overwhelmed him in prison and crushed him beneath a load of debt. Perhaps his doom was just; perhaps it was shamefully unjust; that is not for him to say. However, for the sake of argument, let us concede that he was righteously fined and imprisoned; in that case, can Your Excellency, Governor West, or Your Honor, Chief Justice Zane, who are pledged to observe the impartial execution of the laws, explain why the poor, defenseless and undefended stranger, American citizen as he was, should be even justly mulcted by large fines and then thrown into prison because while editing a Mormon paper he printed some (for the sake of argument) conceded but inadvertent libels, while the anti-Mormon writer of the Salt Lake *Tribune* has been thus far permitted to publish the following blotch on journalism as well as cruel slander with perfect impunity?

The proposition to establish a penal colony on an island of the Northern Sea is a splendid one. There is great wrong in placing the young prisoner convicted of his first offense in company with hardened old scoundrels who have outlived all shame and all self respect, and who, feeling that hope is dead, have but the one desire left, to wreak as much vengeance on society as possible. In point of fact there should be a series of islands occupied on which prisoners might be graded according to the nature of their crimes. Grand larceny thieves would occupy one of the islands; robbers and murderers another; those guilty of bigamy another, etc. This idea receives a new impulse, and the need of an arrangement of the kind is freshly brought to mind by the performances of Hemenway, of the Ogden *Herald*, who has been arraigned on two or three indictments for criminal libel. His paper records the speech that he made a day or two since in behalf of sustaining the demurrers which he had interposed to the complaints against him. This argument reveals the wretch in a new light. He had before clearly established that he was a scoundrel and one of the most brazen of liars; his argument shows that he is besides a cur so dirty that the very idea of insulting prisoners who are only guilty of robbery and bigamy and larceny and such ordinary crimes, by compelling them to bear the unusual punishment of an enforced confinement in Hemenway's society is horrible. The wretch is simply a monster in human form, as cruel as he is cowardly, as brazen as he is depraved. Had Ananias left families by two wives; had the other wife been as accomplished in one peculiar faculty as was Sapphira; had the children of these two families intermarried among themselves and with the most depraved of the world outside; had their masterly ability in one peculiar line increased with each generation for eighteen hundred years, as a measureless and irreclaimable liar Hemenway would have stood off the whole crowd. The cheek of the Frenchman who murdered both his parents and then asked for a full pardon on the ground that he was an orphan, was an exhibition of blushing modesty compared with Hemenway's attempt to establish his innocence of ever having said a disrespectful word of Judge Zane. His pen pictures, as drawn by himself in the *Herald*, of his own appearance when arraigned at the bar of justice, would make a peacock fold his tail and hide under a corn crib or behind the smoke-house. With the forehead of a wolf and the heart of a hyena, he barks vociferously that he never sought to assassinate a good name or to rob a man of his character, and, then, anticipating the swift probability that justice will overtake him, he talks of a possible term in the penitentiary in the same tone that St. Stephen might have used when contemplating martyrdom. We do not believe that the wretch was ever in childhood held on the bosom of a woman or lulled to sleep by a mother's lullaby. Rather we believe he was dropped in an egg in the sand by some reptile and hatched by the east wind, all his attributes are so inhuman. He is simply a mental and moral deformity, so much so, that when we compare him to a reptile or to a spawn of a devilfish we feel like making an abject apology to the saurian and to the octopus. Still, in mercy to the prisoners in the penitentiary, to avoid wounding their self-respect too sorely, we hope, if the jury convicts him, the Court will suspend sentence pending decent behavior, or until the brute, in utter loathing of himself, shall some morning commit hari kari, or until that penal settlement up in the Behring sea shall be established.

Come now, Governor West and Mr. Chief Justice Zane and Gentiles of Ogden, I lay this article, published in your favorite organ, before your judgment and your conscience, and challenge you, each and all, to pronounce it anything but an unmitigated libel under the law of Utah. Whether it be true (as it manifestly cannot be) or false, is it not an atrocious libel still? And why are not both editors served alike? Was the fined and imprisoned editor particularly amenable to extreme punishment because he was poor and defenseless and, by chance, your political antagonist; was the poor, mulcted and incarcerated scribe the more guilty because he, though a Gentile and a native-born American, happened to publish his inadvertent libels in a Mormon paper, through the columns of which he had striven to defend honestly and faithfully not the misdemeanors or crimes of the Mormons, but simply their rights and professed principles of their belief? Or was the *Tribune* writer therefore exempt from all punishment merely because he was rich and influential among those who administer the laws here; and more particularly because he besmirched the character and thus exposed to ostracism a brother writer and fellow American citizen, who perhaps mistakenly, but, withal, conscientiously defended the despised Mormons, even as a lawyer would his client, and who was poor, defenseless and a stranger in Utah? But, mark you! I would not have the editor of the *Tribune* exposed even to the just penalties of his cruel and rancorous assault upon myself, merely out of personal gratification, for I would regret to see even him pained or mulcted, however little, but weightier still is my grief and lamentation to behold, in his peculiar immunity, the debauchery of American justice and the practical destruction of the equality of American citizenship before the law. Yet, more especially, not only in the sacred name of your loyalty to American justice, which is the chief safeguard to the liberty bequeathed us by our revolutionary fathers, but in the name of the sanctity of American motherhood do I call upon, and by virtue of your own love of equity and fatherland, compel Your Excellency and Your Honor and you, ye

Gentiles of Ogden, to consider the following which I re-quote from the editorial columns of the Salt Lake *Tribune* of January, 1886, and either say by your silence that you acquiesce in this dastard attack upon the maternal character of a gray-haired, venerable old lady, tottering upon the brink of the grave, or else speak and act, that an American mother's hitherto unblemished fame may not be hastened in sorrow into the shroud of death, by this wanton black aspersive assumption, which can become nobody, and would deserve no more notice than the hawkings of a blatherskite, had it not been heralded all over the land through the medium of a newspaper:

"We [the *Tribune*] do not believe that the wretch [meaning Hemenway] was ever in childhood held on the bosom of a woman or lulled to sleep by a mother's lullaby. Rather we believe he was dropped in an egg in the sand by some reptile and hatched by the east wind, all his attributes are so inhuman."—*Tribune Editorial, January,* 1886.

By a method of cowardly innuendo the writer of this billingsgate here virtually asserts that my mother was a reptile. In the excess of his hateful malice he can assume that a venerable Gentile American mother like a serpent dropped her offspring as an egg in the sand, and was so devoid of maternal instincts as to allow him to be developed by the east wind of chance; so that it was all her fault because the darker epithets in the category of reproach were to be so viciously applied to him.

In defense of my mother, I lay this matter before you, my most august peers, and in the name of my American birth and citizenship I implore at your hands simply relief from the irreparable injury and ostracism which the above quoted, base *Tribune* calumniations have caused. I have been fined and imprisoned until, in debt and poverty, I am no longer able to think of bearing the expense of prosecuting my persecutor and reviler and my mother's cowardly traducer, at civil suit. Moreover, I want no remuneration for an injury that must ever be irreparable, but I do again, as I have repeatedly done publicly before, beg for such poor relief as the judiciary of Utah can grant by legally branding the calumniations a libel, without further distressing the pitiable man who perpetrated them, beyond the necessary gnawings of remorse which he is sure to feel sooner or later. But whether I now procure redress or not at your hands, I lay this open testamentary letter before my countrymen throughout the United States, in all confidence that they, in good time, will demand a release of the American name from the reproach of such a glaring and pernicious, effectually oppressive and tyrannical, gross inequality of justice as that presented in my case compared with the local legal treatment of the *Tribune* writer. If I erred to the injury of others, I have paid the severe penalty as best I could, and moreover, have I striven to right such errors by every means in my power, but after all this I was no sooner released from prison through the grace of Your Honor, Mr. Chief Justice, than, as yourself can witness, if you have a clear recollection, this *Tribune* writer again poured forth the vials of his vilification upon my crushed and humble person, extending the barriers of ostracism against me, and festering my pathway with thorns.

Fellow citizens, guardians of justice and the laws! say that I do not appeal to your honor, your love of fair play and equity and to your best judgment in vain.

CHARLES W. HEMENWAY.

OGDEN, January 22nd, 1887.

APPENDIX B.

A TOUCHING ADDRESS BEFORE THE FIRST DISTRICT COURT.

WORDS THAT LAY BARE THE ATTITUDE OF INDIVIDUAL MORMONS TOWARDS THE EDMUNDS LAW.

WHEREAS the attitude of Mormons accused of illegal cohabitation is not by any means generally comprehended accurately, I have deemed it of interest to reproduce the address which Mr. F. A. Brown delivered before the First District Court, at Ogden, on the occasion of his trial, June 30th, 1885, on the charge of unlawful cohabitation. Mr. Brown, a venerable, gray-haired man, was permitted to take the witness stand. While under oath he gave the United States Prosecuting Attorney all the testimony necessary to ensure his conviction under the rulings of the Utah courts, and then, while yet under oath, he made use of the following language, every word of which, I am sure, he felt most deeply convicted, was true:

If the Court please:

Notwithstanding I have able counsel to plead my cause, I am happy to have the privilege of speaking a few words in my own defense. I descended from the old Puritan stock of the New England States; the land of early piety and steady habits. My forefathers bravely fought and bled during the ever memorable period—the American Revolution, which brought our national independence and bestowed the rich boon of religious liberty upon their posterity. My parents emigrated from Connecticut to the western portion of the State of New York in the early days, and amid great adversity and the almost insurmountable hardships of a new country, reared a family of ten children, I being the seventh child. I learned in early childhood to love my country, and her great government and institutions, and revere and render strict obedience to all her laws, which I have done from my youth up to the present time. While absent from my dear home and beloved country, sojourning among strangers in foreign lands, I could look with pride upon the flag of my country, as it waved gracefully in the breeze, welcoming the downt-rodden and oppressed of all nations to "the land of the free and the home of the brave"—and call it mine.

I was taught by my parents, and in the Sunday school, to reverence the Holy Bible and receive it as the word of God, and to live according to its precepts. My parents belonged to the Methodist Episcopal Church, and I was traditionated in their doctrines and reared in their faith, until I was twenty-one years of age, when I first heard the fulness of the Gospel of Jesus Christ as revealed through the Prophet Joseph Smith.

I was now old enough to act upon my own agency and think for myself, and after a thorough investigation of the scriptures of divine truth, and the doctrines taught by the Elders of the Church of Jesus Christ of Latter-day Saints, I became convinced; and from an honest conviction of my heart, on the eleventh day of February, A. D. 1844, I yielded obedience to the Gospel of the Son of God, and thereby received a knowledge of its truth, and also the divine mission of Joseph Smith, as Jesus has said: "He that doeth my will shall know of the doctrine whether it be of God or whether it be of man." By embracing an unpopular religion, I was belied and reviled by my relatives, and those who had formerly professed great friendship. In the fall of the same year, I gathered with the Saints at Nauvoo, and suffered with them in their expulsion from that place at the hands of a ruthless mob.

On the fifth day of June, A. D. 1856, I left Council Bluffs (where I resided some six years) for Utah, and arrived here in September following. On the second day of April, A. D. 1857, I accepted of and entered into the holy order of celestial marriage, as revealed through Joseph Smith, from an honest conviction of my heart that it was a pure principle and had emanated from God, and that it was my duty to obey it. I was convinced that if I would be a child of Abraham, I must do the works of Father Abraham and follow the worthy example of all the prophets and holy men of old, who had the divine favor of Almighty God, that I might be worthy to enjoy their society when I pass behind the veil.

Over forty years of my life have been spent in the Church of Jesus Christ of Latter-day Saints, and I have never heard a false doctrine taught during that length of time, or the first wrong counsel given by the leaders of the Church. A more loyal people does not dwell in these United States or in any other portion of the earth.

I have struggled in poverty now nearly thirty long years to provide for my beloved wives and dear children as a fond father and a kind husband should; and I have kept inviolate my solemn vows and most sacred contracts that I made with these women, up to this time to the best of my ability, and, I believe, to their entire satisfaction.

I have as good and respectable a family as any monogomist in the United States or the world, and feel proud of them. My honorable Gentile neighbors, Mr. Read, Mr. Leland, Postmaster Littlefield and others, have never been disgraced by them, and, I think, have never had any cause to be ashamed of them.

I now ask Your Honor what I am to do? Shall I break the most sacred obligations man can enter into, with impunity, and sever the strongest ties of love and affection that have grown up in the human heart between husband and wives, parents and children, to gratify religious bigotry or the spleen of men? Shall I abandon my wives and children (who are as dear to me as Your Honor's, if you have any, are to you, or any other man's wife and children are to him) and cast them off upon the charities of a cold world, and thereby render my wives prostitutes and my children bastards and or phans? Or shall I keep my covenants sacred with my family, like a high-minded, honorable and honest man?

I know not of what metal Your Honor is composed, but, for myself, before I will prove recreant to my wives and children and betray my trust I will suffer my head to be severed from my body.

I have not wronged a man or a woman on earth during

my life that I am aware of. I have trespassed upon no one's rights to my knowledge. This is the first time in my life I have been called upon to answer to a charge of crime against my country's laws. I have either been too shrewd for the officers of the law, or I have proved myself loyal and lived above the law for the past sixty-three years.

Coercion is not known in the marital relations of the Latter-day Saints. They have entered into these holy relations mutually of their own free will and choice, as a vital part of their religion, not to merely imitate the example of the prophets and patriarchs of old, but they have embraced the celestial order of marriage for time and all eternity, because God has revealed it unto them through his prophet, and commanded us to obey it. Your Honor can assign us to prisons and assess fines and even put us to death, but that will only place us beyond your power and put us in possession of the rich blessings God has promised unto us through obedience to His everlasting Gospel.

If Congress can by enactment hinder the free exercise of that part of our religion in taking to ourselves a plurality of wives, and not violate the Constitution of the United States, then Congress can hinder the free exercise of our religion in being baptized for the remission of our sins, the paying of our tithes, the gathering to Zion, or the attending to any other ordinance or requirement of the Gospel of Christ. Our faith is a living faith; for it produces works; hence we show our faith by our works. When it ceases to produce works, it becomes a dead faith; for the Apostle James has declared that "faith without works is dead, being alone." As well might Congress by unconstitutional laws determine the number of children our wives should bear unto us.

If the conscience of the American people is outraged by

my conduct in obeying what my conscience prompts me to be my duty to my God, and demand my liberty, they are welcome to it. Decisions of courts, enactments of Congresses and edicts of tyrants, strike no terror to me, when they come in contact with my known duty to my God. I hope our government and her officers will prove as zealous in the execution of the Edmunds law, in punishing monogamists who cohabit with more than one woman, and cause them to live a life of shame, as they are in prosecuting polygamists who provide for and honor their wives, and rear and educate their children, and thereby prove to the world that they administer the law impartially. If the conscience of the American people demand it, I bow submissively to an unconstitutional law, which Your Honor has the power to execute. I am in your hands, and if Your Honor thinks it will subserve the interests of our country or benefit humanity in any way by inflicting pains and penalties upon me, for doing what I know to be my duty to my God, you can incarcerate me in prison. Prisons nor death itself can not obliterate the knowledge God has given me of His great latter-day work.

I stand here innocent of any known crime; I have a conscience void of offense before God and all men. I am guiltless of violating the law of God or any constitutional law of the land.

Now while you are enjoying your liberty, and the immunities of a free government, and while gamblers, libertines and prostitutes can revel in sin and corruption, without the fear of prosecution or of being deprived of their liberties, please remember me and my brethren whom you are instrumental in depriving of these heaven-born treasures, being innocent of any crime.

While you and yours are enjoying all that is near and dear on earth, supplied with all the comforts and even luxuries of life, please remember the innocent women and children you cause to suffer by tearing from them their only support.

I have made up my mind that while water runs or grass grows, and a drop of blood flows through my veins, or I am permitted to breathe the breath of life, I shall obey the supreme laws of my God in preference to the changeable and imperfect laws of man; and I can only exclaim in the beautiful language of the heroic and patriotic American orator, Patrick Henry, "give me liberty or give me death."

In conclusion I wish to say this to the Court, as you are a stranger among us and ignorant of our doctrines and practices: that we honor and respect you in your position as a representative of our great government. I entertain no malice in my heart towards this court or any of my accusers. I will therefore say to Your Honor before you pass sentence upon me, to consider well all the circumstances connected with my case. I am well known in Ogden City, and have been for the past twenty-eight years, and I defy any man, woman or child to justly accuse me of wronging them.

No one ever heard me take the name of God in vain; no one ever saw me intoxicated. No one ever knew me to patronize houses of ill-fame or gambling dens. I have lived above reproach and set a Christian example before my family and all the world, and no one can justly accuse me of violating the laws of my country or of committing any crime, unless it is a crime to love my wives and children. If I have embraced an error in my religion, come to me in the spirit of the Gospel and point it out, taking the word of God that you profess to believe in, and show me any portion of my faith false and I will renounce it; and if you will present me something better than I already have, I will accept it gladly.

I know the doctrines that are preached by the Latter-day Saints are the pure Gospel of the Son of God. For this knowledge I am not dependent upon the testimony of Joseph Smith, Brigham Young, John Taylor or any other man. I have obtained this knowledge for myself through the revelations of Jesus Christ unto me. With what measure you mete unto others it shall be measured unto you again.

I expect to stand before the bar of God, in the court above, and give an account of the deeds done in the body, and if I cannot obtain my rights in the courts on earth, I have no fears but that I shall receive equity and justice at the hands of God in heaven, and I can afford to wait. I would to God that not only this court, but also all who are interested in persecuting the Saints of God, and all who hear me this day were both almost and altogether such as I am, except my bonds.

May God have mercy upon this Court, and all who are engaged in this unholy crusade against an honest, virtuous, industrious and God-fearing people. This is all I wish to say at present, thanking you for your kind indulgence.

F. A. Brown.

The subscriber of the above address (which we give exactly as it was read in court) is not what would be called a Mormon leader. He is, however, a fair representative of the masses of the unfortunate Mormons who have been prosecuted under the Edmunds law. His sentiments and views are those of the mass of the whole Mormon people. I know him to be all he claims to be; a man whose word no one, who is acquainted with him, would for a moment doubt on an ordinary topic. How can any government justly, or at all, suppress the conscientious practices of such men by any legal means? is a question that Congress and the people of the United States ought to consider carefully before they proceed to inflict further legal punishments upon the Mormons.

CHARLES W. HEMENWAY.

www.ingramcontent.com/pod-product-compliance
Lightning Source LLC
Chambersburg PA
CBHW031948230426
43672CB00010B/2094